ARCHITECTS OF THE INFORMATION AGE

COMPUTING AND CONNECTING IN THE 21ST CENTURY

ARCHITECTS OF THE INFORMATION AGE

EDITED BY ROBERT CURLEY, MANAGER, SCIENCE AND TECHNOLOGY

Britannica
Educational Publishing

IN ASSOCIATION WITH

ROSEN
EDUCATIONAL SERVICES

Published in 2012 by Britannica Educational Publishing
(a trademark of Encyclopædia Britannica, Inc.)
in association with Rosen Educational Services, LLC
29 East 21st Street, New York, NY 10010.

First Edition

Britannica Educational Publishing
Michael I. Levy: Executive Editor
J.E. Luebering: Senior Manager
Marilyn L. Barton: Senior Coordinator, Production Control
Steven Bosco: Director, Editorial Technologies
Lisa S. Braucher: Senior Producer and Data Editor
Yvette Charboneau: Senior Copy Editor
Kathy Nakamura: Manager, Media Acquisition
Robert Curley : Manager, Science and Technology

Rosen Educational Services
Heather M. Moore Niver: Editor
Nelson Sá: Art Director
Cindy Reiman: Photography Manager
Matthew Cauli: Designer, Cover Design
Introduction by Greg Roza

Library of Congress Cataloging-in-Publication Data

Architects of the information age / edited by Robert Curley.—1st ed.
    p. cm.—(Computing and connecting in the 21st century)
"In association with Britannica Educational Publishing, Rosen Educational Services."
Includes bibliographical references and index.
ISBN 978-1-61530-661-9 (library binding)
1. Computer scientists—Biography. 2. Telecommunications engineers—Biography. I.
Curley, Robert, 1955-
QA76.2.A2A73 2012
004.092'2—dc23
[B]

                                                              2011015174

Manufactured in the United States of America

On the cover: Clockwise from top left are Sean Parker, Steve Jobs, Mark Zuckerberg, Meg
Whitman, and Bill Gates, each of whom has made groundbreaking contributions to the
world of computerized communication. *Miguel Villagran/Getty Images (Parker), Shaun Curry/
AFP/Getty Images (Jobs), Mandel Ngan/AFP/Getty Images (Zuckerberg), Frederick M. Brown/
Getty Images (Whitman), Scott Gries/Getty Images (Gates)*

On pages x-xi: The creativity and inventive thinking of countless inventors over the years
have resulted in ever more advanced computers and technology. *Hemera/Thinkstock*

Page iii © www.istockphoto.com/Falk Kienas; pp. v, vi, vii, viii, xi (background graphic)
© www.istockphoto.com/Simfo; pp. 2, 30, 93, 96, 108, 126 © www.istockphoto.com/Karl
Dolenc; pp. 5, 12, 15, 18, 24, 26, 34, 40, 44, 48, 59, 71, 73, 80, 82, 85, 114, 117, 135, 137, 144 © www.
istockphoto.com/Johan Ramberg; pp. 35, 36, 37, 64, 65, 70, 100, 101, 120, 121, 138, 139 © www.
istockphoto.com/Andrey Volodin; remaining interior background image Yoshikazu Tsuno/
AFP/Getty Images

CONTENTS

96

108

114

INTRODUCTION

Computers have come to rule nearly every facet of our modern world. From alarm clocks to automobiles, computer technology has revolutionized the way people live their lives. Thanks to the Internet, satellites, laptops, and cell phones, we have the potential to converse with anyone anywhere in the world in an instant. Despite the flourishing of computer technology in a relatively short period of time, few people stop to think about the pioneers and innovators who helped bring about the computer revolution.

While modern computers began to take shape in the 1950s, the roots of computer technology extend back to 1790. That was the year French inventor Joseph-Marie Jacquard came up with an idea that transformed the textile industry. Data in the form of cards with holes punched in them were fed into Jacquard's loom. The cards told the loom what designs to weave.

The use of punch cards influenced other scientists, notably English mathematician Charles Babbage. In 1837 Babbage described the Analytical Engine, which used Jacquard's card-reading technology to solve mathematical calculations. Babbage's machine could print out answers and even create new punch cards to store data for future use.

Countess Ada Lovelace — a friend of Babbage's — wrote an algorithm intended to be processed by the machine. Today, many consider Babbage's design to be the first plans for a digital computer and Ada Lovelace to be the first computer programmer.

Jacquard's punch cards also inspired American inventor Herman Hollerith. Hollerith developed a machine that read and sorted punch cards to tabulate the U.S. census of 1890. In the following years, Hollerith founded the Tabulating Machine Company to manufacture the punch card machines.

In 1924, after a series of mergers, Hollerith's company transformed into the International Business Machines Corporation (IBM). Led by Thomas Watson, Sr. — and later by his son, Thomas Watson, Jr. — IBM became a world leader in the manufacture of electric typewriters and calculators. Today IBM is one of the leading computer manufacturers in the world.

In the early 1900s, several notable mathematicians, engineers, and scientists laid the groundwork for the computer revolution that would soon follow. Engineer Vannevar Bush developed analog computers to help strengthen the nation's military and electric-power network. In 1945 Bush wrote a paper on a device capable of archiving, indexing, retrieving, and cross-referencing data. This idea foreshadowed the advent of hypertext and the World Wide Web.

In the late 1930s physicist John Atanasoff, along with electrical engineer Clifford Berry, invented the Atanasoff-Berry Computer. This machine could solve complex problems using data expressed in binary form. More than 30 years later it was recognized as the first digital computer.

Grace Murray Hopper was a rear admiral in the U.S. Navy, but she was also a brilliant mathematician. She helped develop the first large-scale automatic calculator, a forerunner to the first electronic computers. She is perhaps best remembered for creating the first compiler— software that translates source code written by a programmer into a language understood by computers. Hopper also coined the phrase *bug* to refer to computer glitches.

Throughout the next few decades, scientists strove to create smaller but more powerful computers. They were aided by inventors like William B. Shockley, who made the first transistor. The brilliant British mathematician Alan Turing became a pioneer in both digital computer design and artificial intelligence. American electrical engineer Claude Shannon developed the theoretical foundation of digital circuits.

In 1946 American inventors John Mauchly and J. Presper Eckert created the first general-purpose, completely electronic digital computer: the Electronic Numerical Integrator and Computer (ENIAC). This machine was the most powerful computer built to date, but it was enormous, taking up much of a 30-by-50-foot (15-by-9-metre) basement of the Moore School of Electrical Engineering at the University of Pennsylvania.

In the late 1940s British inventor Tom Kilburn, along with Frederick Williams, built the first computer memory system and the first stored-program computer. Kilburn would go on to develop virtual memory and use it to create more and more powerful computers.

In 1949 Maurice Wilkes and others built the Electronic Delay Storage Automatic Calculator (EDSAC), the first full-sized stored-program computer. Wilkes's work on EDSAC and other computers introduced the concept of microprogramming to the world. This allowed computer programs to be stored on the computer itself. Wilkes also introduced the concept of cache memory for faster processing.

With the invention of the basic computer hardware other inventers and scientists began making leaps and bounds in the world of computer technology. American inventor Douglas Englebart introduced the world to the computer mouse, multiple-window display, and hypermedia. Inspired by the writings of Vannevar Bush, Englebart laid the groundwork for the development of graphical user interface (GUI) computer programs, which quickly made computer operation easier and more natural for users.

In the late 1950s American inventors, including Robert Noyce and Jack Kilby, began making great progress with more powerful transistors. While working for different companies, both men began creating computer circuitry on silicon wafers, giving birth to the integrated circuit. Noyce, however, took the process even further.

Noyce and several colleagues founded the Intel Corporation in 1968. In 1971, Intel introduced the first microprocessor: a single silicon chip that contained the circuitry necessary for both computer processing and computer storage. This was a major step forward on the route to the mass production of personal computers.

In the late 1960s computer scientist Vinton Cerf and electrical engineer Robert Kahn were two members of the American team working on a new type of computer network called ARPANET (Advanced Research Projects Agency Network). This network, which first consisted of four "nodes," or computer centres spread across the United States, was the first to use packet switching (in which messages were divided into many "packets" that moved separately over numerous different circuits to their common destination) to send information more quickly than ever before.

Cerf helped Kahn design the new network, which was successfully tested in 1969. Together, Cerf and Kahn created the protocols—sets of rules for transmitting data between electronic devices—needed for computers to communicate over long distances. Less than two years later the first e-mail system was successfully tested on ARPANET. The work of Cerf and Kahn and the other members of their team would soon change the world as the Internet came into being.

In 1969 Dennis Ritchie and Ken Thomson created a flexible computer operating system (OS) that, unlike those that had come before it, was not completely tied to any particular computer hardware. They called it UNIX. Even today, UNIX is well known for its portability, or the ability to function on different systems. However, when Ritchie and Thomson first tried to move UNIX from the original system to a new one, they encountered problems with the programming language they created for it. In response Ritchie created the C programming language, which has since become one of the most popular programming languages of all time. The C programming language has influenced the creation of many other programming languages, including C++ and Java.

Computer scientist Charles Thacker led the team at Xerox Palo Alto Research Center that created the first personal computer, called Alto, in 1973. Alto could display several "windows" on its screen, each of which could be manipulated by a computer mouse. Alto was so expensive to manufacture that the Xerox company decided not to market the computer, believing that too few would be able to buy it. Thacker went on to help develop Ethernet, a popular computer networking technology used in local area networks (LANs).

In the late 1970s, two enterprising young computer engineers, Stephen Wozniak and Steven Jobs, founded

Apple Computer Inc. (later Apple Inc.). They sold their personal belongings to get their company off the ground and started the company in Jobs's garage, quickly building a name for themselves as the personal computer market took off. In 1977 Wozniak and Jobs created the first successfully marketable personal computer: the Apple II. They created a personal computer that was both functional and eye-catching. The Apple II was an instant success. In just four years Jobs and Wozniak became multimillionaires.

In the years that followed, Apple went though many changes and designed more groundbreaking products. Both Wozniak and Jobs eventually left Apple, but continued to be major players in the development of personal computers. In 1997 Apple was in financial trouble and needed to develop a new operating system. Jobs came back to lead the company once more, reviving Apple with the trendy and stylish iMac personal computers. Before his 2011 resignation as CEO of Apple, Jobs continued to innovate, and followed with more groundbreaking technology, including the iBook laptop, the iPod portable MP3 player, the iPhone, and the iPad tablet computer.

At about the same time Wozniak and Jobs were preparing to assemble the Apple II, a young computer programmer named Bill Gates began developing software. Dropping out of Harvard University in his junior year, Gates founded Microsoft, a software company. Gates designed an operating system called MS-DOS, which he licensed to IBM for use in its first microcomputer, the IBM PC. Gate's software quickly became the industry standard for PC operating systems. By the mid-1980s Gates became a billionaire.

In 1985, Microsoft introduced a new type of operating system, based on Apple concepts, called Windows. It allowed users to view multiple folders, or windows, on a virtual desktop. As the Internet gained popularity in the early 1990s, Microsoft continued to lead the software industry with new designs. Microsoft released Windows 95 in 1995. It was a revolutionary operating system that integrated the Windows and MS-DOS operating systems and offered built-in Internet support. Using the Microsoft Web browser Internet Explorer, both PC and Apple computer users could easily surf the Web. Windows transformed rapidly into the world's most-used operating system.

While Jobs, Wozniak, and Gates are the figures largely credited with shaping the current personal computer industry, many other innovators contributed to the burgeoning technology. Computer programmer Richard Stallman started the Free Software Foundation in 1985. The initial purpose of this foundation was to create a free version of the UNIX operating system. Stallman called his operating system GNU, and it was used to create a set of free computer software that has come to be used by numerous programmers and companies. Stallman and the Free Software Foundation created the GNU General Public License (GNU GPL), which grants people the right to freely use, modify, and distribute software that would normally be protected by copyright laws. Today numerous open-source resources have adopted the GNU GPL.

Other innovators were also interested in creating free software, including Finnish computer programmer Linus Torvalds, who created the Linux operating system kernel in 1991. Torvalds released the Linux kernel as an open-source code. It quickly became known as a dependable alternative to Windows and Macintosh operating systems. Several of Stallman's GNU utilities were combined with the Linux kernel to create the GNU/Linux operating system in 1994.

Thanks to the continuing efforts of inventors and innovators, the Internet has become a rich new world where enterprising individuals can host exciting resources for the public. In 1998 Stanford University graduates Sergey Brin and Larry Page founded a search engine company called Google Inc. By 2004 Google had become the most powerful search engine on the Internet, and Brin and Page had become billionaires. Also that year Google began offering Gmail, a free Web-based e-mail account. Today, about 70 percent of all searches are handled by Google.

In February 2004 Harvard student Mark Zuckerberg created thefacebook.com (renamed Facebook in 2005), which enabled his fellow students to share personal information and photos. Within two weeks half of the students enrolled at Harvard had signed up. Zuckerberg and his friends added features and made the site available to students on campuses across the country. In the summer of 2004 Zuckerberg dropped out of Harvard and moved his headquarters to Palo Alto, Calif. Facebook grew into the biggest social networking site in the world.

The development of computer technology—from Jacquard's loom to Zuckerberg's Facebook—has rapidly revolutionized the way our world functions. With creative inventors and programmers leading the way, this technology is sure to keep evolving. What do the computer scientists of tomorrow have in store for us? Surely we won't have long to wait.

CHAPTER 1

JOSEPH-MARIE JACQUARD

Born July 7, 1752, Lyon, France—died Aug. 7, 1834, Oullins, France.

Joseph-Marie Jacquard of France was the inventor of the Jacquard loom, a machine employing punched cards that created a technological revolution in the textile industry. Jacquard's invention became the basis of the modern automatic loom, and it is also seen as the first example of a machine that could be directed to perform different tasks by feeding it instructions from a predetermined program.

Jacquard first formed the idea for his loom in 1790, but his work was cut short by the French Revolution, in which he fought on the side of the Revolutionaries in the defense of Lyon. In 1801 Jacquard demonstrated an improved drawloom, for which he was awarded a bronze medal. He continued his work, and in 1804–05 he introduced an attachment that has caused any loom that uses it to be called a Jacquard loom. Jacquard's loom used interchangeable punched cards that controlled the weaving of the cloth so that any desired pattern could be obtained automatically. It enabled looms to produce fabrics having intricate woven patterns such as tapestry, brocade, and damask, and it was also adapted to the production of patterned knitted fabrics.

In 1806 the loom was declared public property, and Jacquard was rewarded with a pension and a royalty on each machine. However, the loom aroused bitter hostility among the silk weavers, who feared that its labour-saving capabilities would deprive them of jobs.

The Jacquard loom used punched cards to create patterns in weaving. Punched cards were eventually used to input data in early computers. Henry Guttmann/Hulton Archive/Getty Images

The weavers of Lyon not only burned machines that were put into production but attacked Jacquard as well. Eventually, the advantages of the loom brought about its general acceptance, and by 1812 there were 11,000 in use in France. In 1819 Jacquard was awarded a gold medal and the Cross of the Legion of Honour. The use of his loom spread to England in the 1820s and from there virtually worldwide.

Jacquard's punched cards, containing a set of instructions for running a machine, essentially transformed his loom into the first practical information-processing device. In the 19th century, punched cards were adopted by the noted English inventor Charles Babbage as an input-output medium for his proposed Analytical Engine, and they were used by the American statistician Herman Hollerith to feed data to his census machine. In the 20th century, punched cards were used as a means of inputting data into early digital computers.

CHAPTER 2

CHARLES BABBAGE

Born Dec. 26, 1791, London, Eng.—died Oct. 18, 1871, London.

Charles Babbage was an English mathematician and inventor who, in the first half of the 19th century, is credited with having conceived the first automatic digital computer. In 1812 Babbage helped found the Analytical Society, whose object was to introduce developments from the European continent into English mathematics. In 1816 he was elected a fellow of the Royal Society of London. He was instrumental in founding the Royal Astronomical (1820) and Statistical (1834) societies.

The idea of mechanically calculating mathematical tables first came to Babbage in 1812 or 1813. Later he made a small calculator that could perform certain mathematical computations to eight decimals. Then in 1823 he obtained government support for the design of the Difference Engine, a projected machine with a 20-decimal capacity. Because its construction required the development of mechanical engineering techniques, Babbage devoted himself to working them out. Owing to various technical difficulties, the machine was never finished, and construction ended in 1833. In the meantime (1828–39), Babbage served as Lucasian Professor of Mathematics at the University of Cambridge.

During the mid-1830s Babbage developed plans for the Analytical Engine, which was to be a general-purpose, fully program-controlled, automatic mechanical digital computer. In this device Babbage envisioned the

In 1991, for the 200th anniversary of Babbage's birth, his Difference Engine No. 2 was built to his specifications. SSPL via Getty Images

capability of performing any arithmetical operation on the basis of instructions from punched cards, a memory unit in which to store numbers, sequential control, and most of the other basic elements of the present-day computer. However, the Analytical Engine, like the Difference Engine before it, was never completed. A portion of the "mill" (the calculating unit, corresponding to the central processing unit of a modern computer), built for demonstration purposes before Babbage's death, is on display in the Science Museum in London.

While working on plans for the Analytical Engine, Babbage also designed a simplified version of his Difference Engine that would be accurate to 31 digits. Now known as the Difference Engine No. 2, this machine was built to Babbage's specifications by a group at the Science Museum between 1985 and 2002. The mill was completed, and shown to work as Babbage had projected, in time for the 200th anniversary of his birth in 1991.

Babbage made notable contributions in other areas as well. He helped establish the modern postal system in England and compiled the first reliable actuarial tables. He also invented a type of speedometer and the locomotive cowcatcher.

CHAPTER 3

LADY LOVELACE

Born Dec. 10, 1815, Piccadilly Terrace, Middlesex [now in London], Eng.—died Nov. 29, 1852, Marylebone, London.

Ada King, countess of Lovelace, was an English mathematician and an associate of Charles Babbage, for whose prototype of a digital computer she created a program. She has been called the first computer programmer.

She was born Augusta Ada Byron, the daughter of famed poet Lord Byron and Annabella Milbanke Byron, who legally separated two months after her birth. Her father then left Britain forever, and his daughter never knew him personally. The young Lady Byron was educated privately by tutors and then self-educated but was helped in her advanced studies by mathematician-logician Augustus De Morgan, the first professor of mathematics at the University of London. On

Ada King, countess of Lovelace. SSPL via Getty Images

July 8, 1835, she married William King, 8th Baron King. When he was created an earl in 1838, she became countess of Lovelace.

She became interested in Babbage's machines as early as 1833 and, most notably, in 1843 came to translate and annotate an article written by the Italian mathematician and engineer Luigi Federico Menabrea, "Notions sur la machine analytique de Charles Babbage" (1842; "Elements of Charles Babbage's Analytical Machine"). Her detailed and elaborate annotations (especially her description of how the proposed Analytical Engine could be programmed to compute Bernoulli numbers) were excellent. "The Analytical Engine," she said, "weaves algebraic patterns, just as the Jacquard-loom weaves flowers and leaves."

CHAPTER 4

GEORGE BOOLE

Born Nov. 2, 1815, Lincoln, Lincolnshire, Eng.—died Dec. 8, 1864, Ballintemple, County Cork, Ire.

G eorge Boole was an English mathematician who helped establish modern symbolic logic. His algebra of logic, now called Boolean algebra, is basic to the design of digital computer circuits.

Boole was given his first lessons in mathematics by his father, a tradesman, who also taught him to make optical instruments. Aside from his father's help and a few years at local schools, however, Boole was self-taught in mathematics. When his father's business declined, George had to work to support the family. From the age of 16 he taught in village schools in the West Riding of Yorkshire, and he opened his own school in Lincoln when he was 20. During scant leisure time he read mathematics journals in the Lincoln's Mechanics Institute. There he also read Isaac Newton's *Principia*, Pierre-Simon Laplace's *Traité de mécanique céleste*, and Joseph-Louis Lagrange's *Mécanique analytique* and began to solve advanced problems in algebra.

Boole submitted a stream of original papers to the new *Cambridge Mathematical Journal*, beginning in 1839 with his "Researches on the Theory of Analytical Transformations." These papers were on differential equations and the algebraic problem of linear transformation, emphasizing the concept of invariance. In 1844, in an important paper in the *Philosophical Transactions of the*

Royal Society for which he was awarded the Royal Society's first gold medal for mathematics, he discussed how methods of algebra and calculus might be combined. Boole soon saw that his algebra could also be applied in logic.

Developing novel ideas on logical method and confident in the symbolic reasoning he had derived from his mathematical investigations, he published in 1847 a pamphlet, "Mathematical Analysis of Logic," in which he argued persuasively that logic should be allied with mathematics, not philosophy. He won the admiration of the English logician Augustus De Morgan, who published *Formal Logic* the same year. On the basis of his publications, in 1849 Boole was appointed professor of mathematics at Queen's College, County Cork, even though he lacked a university degree. In 1854 he published *An Investigation into the Laws of Thought, on Which Are Founded the Mathematical Theories of Logic and Probabilities*, which he regarded as a mature statement of his ideas. The next year he married Mary Everest, niece of Sir George Everest, for whom the mountain is named. The Booles had five daughters.

One of the first Englishmen to write on logic, Boole pointed out the analogy between algebraic symbols and those that can represent logical forms and syllogisms, showing how the symbols of quantity can be separated from those of operation. With Boole in 1847 and 1854 began the algebra of logic, or what is now called Boolean algebra. Boole's original and remarkable general symbolic method of logical inference, fully stated in *Laws of Thought* (1854), enables one, given any propositions involving any number of terms, to draw conclusions that are logically contained in the premises. He also attempted a general method in probabilities, which would make it possible from the given probabilities of any system of events to determine the consequent probability of any other event logically connected with the given events.

In 1857 Boole was elected a fellow of the Royal Society. The influential *Treatise on Differential Equations* appeared in 1859 and was followed the next year by its sequel, *Treatise on the Calculus of Finite Differences*. Used as textbooks for many years, these works embody an elaboration of Boole's more important discoveries. Boole's abstruse reasoning has led to applications of which he never dreamed: for example, telephone switching and electronic computers use binary digits and logical elements that rely on Boolean logic for their design and operation.

CHAPTER 5

HERMAN HOLLERITH

Born Feb. 29, 1860, Buffalo, N.Y., U.S.—died Nov. 17, 1929, Washington, D.C., U.S.

Herman Hollerith was an American inventor of a tabulating machine that was an important precursor of the electronic computer.

Immediately after graduation from the Columbia University School of Mines in 1879, Hollerith became an assistant to his teacher William P. Trowbridge in the U.S.

The Hollerith tabulating machine was a significant predecessor to the electronic computer. SSPL via Getty Images

census of 1880. During the next decade he taught briefly at the Massachusetts Institute of Technology, Cambridge; experimented on air brakes; and worked for the Patent Office in Washington, D.C. Throughout this time he was occupied with the problem of automating the tabulation work of the census. By the time of the census of 1890, he had invented machines to record statistics by electrically reading and sorting punched cards that had been numerically encoded by perforation position. The invention was a success in the United States but drew much more attention in Europe, where it was widely adopted for a number of statistical purposes. In 1896 Hollerith organized the Tabulating Machine Company, incorporated in New York, to manufacture the machines. Through subsequent mergers, most notably under the guidance of Thomas J. Watson, Sr., it grew into the International Business Machines Corporation (IBM).

CHAPTER 6

THOMAS WATSON, SR., AND THOMAS WATSON, JR.

Respectively, born Feb. 17, 1874, Campbell, N.Y., U.S.—died June 19, 1956, New York, N.Y., U.S.; born Jan. 8, 1914, Dayton, Ohio, U.S.—died Dec. 31, 1993, Greenwich, Conn., U.S.

Thomas John Watson, Sr., and his son, Thomas John Watson, Jr., were American industrialists who built the International Business Machines Corporation (IBM) into the largest manufacturer of data-processing equipment in the world. Thomas Watson, Sr., built the company into a leading manufacturer of punch-card tabulating systems and electric typewriters, and Thomas Watson, Jr., after inheriting leadership of the company from his father, propelled it into the computer age.

Thomas Watson, Sr., was the son of a lumber dealer. He studied at the Elmira (N.Y.) School of Commerce and then worked as a salesman first in a retail store and then for a small cash register company. In 1895 Watson joined the sales staff of the National Cash Register Company in Dayton, Ohio, and he eventually rose to the post of general sales manager of the company under the tutelage of its president, John H. Patterson. In 1912 Patterson involved Watson in an illegal antitrust scheme that resulted in convictions for both men, later overturned. Leaving National Cash Register in 1913, Watson in 1914 became president of the Computing-Tabulating-Recording Co., a maker of electrical punch-card computing systems and other products. (The company changed its name to International Business Machines Corporation in 1924.)

An exceptional salesman and organizer, Watson assembled a highly motivated, well-trained, and well-paid staff. He gave pep talks, enforced a strict dress code, and posted the now famous slogan "Think" in company offices. Coupled with an aggressive research and development program, these efforts enabled IBM to dominate its market. Watson aggressively pursued international trade in the 1930s and '40s, extending IBM's virtual monopoly of the business-machines industry worldwide.

In 1952 he turned the IBM presidency over to his son, Thomas, Jr., while retaining the post of chairman. By the time of Watson's death four years later, the company (which had 235 employees in 1914) employed 60,000 people and had 200 offices throughout the country, with factories and assembly plants around the world. Watson

Although International Business Machines (IBM) entered the computer race comparatively late, in the early 1950s it released its first automated systems.

was active in civic affairs and was noted for his efforts on behalf of the arts and world peace.

After graduating (1937) from Brown University, Providence, R.I., Thomas Watson, Jr., joined IBM as a junior salesman while his father presided at the company's helm. In 1946, after returning from World War II service in the Army Air Forces, he quickly moved through the ranks at IBM, becoming a vice president in that year, executive vice president in 1949, and finally president in 1952 (as his father became chairman). The younger Watson ardently pushed for the company to reach beyond tabulating machines and enter the nascent computer industry. IBM finally did so, though later than its rivals; IBM's first large automated system (the IBM 701) was unveiled in 1952. In 1956 Watson became chairman when his father retired. (The elder Watson died six weeks later.) Watson's aggressive tactics and heavy outlays for research established IBM's dominance in the industry so thoroughly that the U.S. government filed an antitrust suit against the company in 1969. (The case was dropped in 1982.) By the time Watson retired in 1971, IBM's stock had increased in value by more than $36 billion from when he gained the chairmanship.

Watson later—from 1979 to 1981—served as ambassador to the Soviet Union. In his memoirs, *Father, Son & Co.* (1990; with Peter Petre), Watson detailed his often stormy relationship with his father.

CHAPTER 7

VANNEVAR BUSH

Born March 11, 1890, Everett, Mass., U.S.—died June 28, 1974, Belmont, Mass., U.S.

Vannevar Bush was an American electrical engineer and administrator who developed the Differential Analyzer and oversaw government mobilization of scientific research during World War II.

Bush received his bachelor's and master's degrees in mathematics from Tufts College (Medford, Mass.) in 1913 and a doctorate in electrical engineering that was awarded jointly by the Massachusetts Institute of Technology (MIT), then located in Boston, and Harvard University, in nearby Cambridge, in 1916. Bush returned to Tufts as an instructor in the fall of 1916 and became involved in antisubmarine research during World War I.

In 1919 Bush joined the electrical engineering department at MIT. During the 1920s and '30s, he and his research laboratory became the preeminent designers and builders of analog computers. (Analog computers represent data with some physical quantity, such as voltage, that is allowed to vary continuously. In contrast, digital computers only allow a discrete set of values for data, typically by using two voltage levels, off and on, to represent the binary numbers, 0 and 1.) Originally developed to solve complex problems associated with long-distance power lines, Bush's analog computers were also applied to many other engineering problems. By 1931 his most successful machine, known as the Differential Analyzer, was operational. Using a complicated arrangement of gears and cams driven by

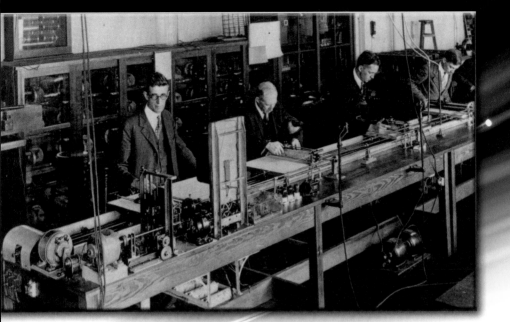

Vannevar Bush (left). General Photographic Agency/Hulton Archive/
Getty Images

steel shafts, the Differential Analyzer could obtain practical (albeit approximate) solutions to problems which up to that point had been prohibitively difficult.

The Differential Analyzer was such a great success that it and various copies located at other laboratories were soon employed in solving diverse engineering and physics problems. An even more successful machine, the so-called Rockefeller Differential Analyzer (funded in part by the Rockefeller Foundation), was built in 1935 and proved the most powerful computer available before the arrival of digital computers in about 1945. It was enlisted by the military in World War II to produce ballistics tables.

In 1939 Bush left MIT for Washington, D.C., where he became president of the Carnegie Institution, the oldest private research institution in America. With the German invasion of Poland in September 1939, Bush approached Pres. Franklin Delano Roosevelt about forming an organization, the National Defense Research Committee (NDRC), to organize research of interest to the military and to inform the armed services about new technologies. The NDRC was formed with Bush as its chairman on June 27, 1940. One year later, the Office of Scientific Research and Development (OSRD) was created with Bush as its chairman. Besides overseeing the NDRC and other science committees, the OSRD functioned as a liaison office among the Allies. By the war's end its annual budget exceeded $500 billion.

Of the many weapons developed through the OSRD, radar and the atomic bomb were prime examples of Bush's managerial and political skills. Through the establishment of the Microwave Committee and the Radiation Laboratory at MIT, Bush created institutions to shepherd the development of microwave-based radar systems—a vast improvement on the long-wave radar systems developed by the U.S. Navy during the 1930s. In turn, these institutions drew upon his MIT connections. Bush's former students and colleagues brought not only their expertise but also networks of researchers at universities such as Stanford and corporations such as the Sperry Gyroscope Company who were developing microwave technology. Bush's prewar connections became an integral aspect of the wartime organization of research—as well as one reason why MIT was the largest single recipient of OSRD contracts.

The atomic bomb displayed another aspect of Bush's leadership. The NDRC, and then the OSRD, absorbed the Uranium Committee that Roosevelt had established in 1939. Dissatisfied with the pace of the committee, Bush added new members. When that committee produced a report claiming that an atomic bomb might not be possible, he quickly convened another committee, armed it with different information, and received the report he wanted: one that stated that a bomb was possible and that Germany was most likely ahead of the United States in its development. He accomplished all this before the United States was attacked by Japan; in doing so, he set in motion the activities that would culminate in the destruction of Hiroshima and Nagasaki in 1945.

Recognizing that science would have a new place in the nation's postwar political culture, Bush delivered to Pres. Harry S. Truman in July 1945 a report titled *Science: The Endless Frontier*, his blueprint for organizing government support of university-based research. Central to Bush's vision was a National Research Foundation (NRF) run by an independently appointed chairman that would fund research for the physical and biological sciences as well as national defense. The defeat of this proposal marked the beginning of the end for Bush's influence on the development of science policy. Fearful of military control of scientific research, Bush published a work of both practical politics and political theory, *Modern Arms and Free Men*, in 1949. Widely discussed and reviewed, the book was Bush's warning that the militarization of American science would harm the development of the economy.

Today Bush is also remembered as a prophet in another field, computer science. In a 1945 article entitled "As We May Think," published in the *Atlantic Monthly*, Bush proposed a device that he called the Memex—an indexed, archival, microfilm machine for cross-referencing and retrieving information. For Bush, this article was an extension of his work in analog computing and microfilm technology. To the modern reader it portends the creation of hypertext and the World Wide Web by Tim Berners-Lee.

CHAPTER 8

JOHN VINCENT ATANASOFF

Born Oct. 4, 1903, Hamilton, N.Y., U.S. — died June 15, 1995, Frederick, Md., U.S.

John Vincent Atanasoff was a physicist who was belatedly credited (in 1973) with developing the first electronic digital computer in the late 1930s. That acknowledgment followed a lawsuit that resulted in a judge's voiding a patent owned by Sperry Rand Corp. on the Electronic Numerical Integrator and Computer (ENIAC), an invention that had been recognized as the first American electronic digital computer. Though Atanasoff gained legal stature for his achievement, many historians continue to credit ENIAC's inventors, J. Presper Eckert, Jr., and John W. Mauchly, as the founding fathers of the modern computer in the United States.

Atanasoff received his B.S. in electrical engineering from the University of Florida, Gainesville, in 1925, his master's degree in mathematics from Iowa State College (now Iowa State University) in 1926, and his Ph.D. in physics from the University of Wisconsin in 1930. After returning to Iowa State to teach mathematics and physics, he developed, with his graduate assistant Clifford Berry, the Atanasoff-Berry Computer (1937–42). The limited-function vacuum-tube device lacked a central processing unit and was not programmable but could solve differential equations using binary arithmetic. Though never finished, the machine was historically important because it contained design components of what would become the basic architecture of a computer. The computer controversy stemmed from a 1941 visit that Mauchly made to Atanasoff and their discussion about the design of the ABC.

Atanasoff abandoned his computer work during World War II to become chief of the acoustics division of the Naval Ordnance Laboratory, Washington, D.C. In 1946 he participated in the atomic bomb tests at Bikini Atoll. In 1952 he established the Ordnance Engineering Co., which he later sold to Aerojet Engineering Corp. He remained with Aerojet until retiring in 1961. He was the recipient in 1981 of the Computer Pioneer Medal and was honoured in 1990 with the National Medal of Technology.

CHAPTER 9

GRACE HOPPER

Born Dec. 9, 1906, New York, N.Y., U.S.—died Jan. 1, 1992, Arlington, Va., U.S.

Grace Brewster Murray Hopper was an American mathematician and rear admiral in the U.S. Navy who was a pioneer in developing computer technology. She helped to devise UNIVAC I, the first commercial electronic computer, and naval applications for the programming language COBOL (*c*ommon-*b*usiness-*o*riented *l*anguage).

After graduating from Vassar College (B.A., 1928), Hopper attended Yale University (M.A., 1930; Ph.D., 1934). She taught mathematics at Vassar before joining the Naval Reserve in 1943. She became a lieutenant and was assigned to the Bureau of Ordnance's Computation Project at Harvard University (1944), where she worked on the Harvard Mark I, the first large-scale automatic calculator and a precursor of electronic computers. She remained at Harvard as a civilian research fellow while maintaining her naval career as a reservist. After a moth infiltrated the circuits of the Mark I, she coined the term *bug* to refer to unexplained computer failures.

In 1949 Hopper joined the Eckert-Mauchly Computer Corp., where she designed an improved compiler, a program that translates a programmer's instructions into computer codes. She remained with the firm when it was taken over by Remington Rand (1951) and by Sperry Rand Corp. (1955). In 1957 her division developed Flow-Matic, the first English-language data-processing compiler. She

Grace Hopper worked on the Harvard Mark I, the first large-scale automatic calculator. PhotoQuest/Archive Photos/Getty Images

retired from the navy with the rank of commander in 1966, but she was recalled to active duty the following year to help standardize the navy's computer languages. When she retired again in 1986 at the age of 79, she was the oldest officer on active U.S. naval duty. She was elected a fellow of the Institute of Electrical and Electronic Engineers (1962), named the first computer science Man of the Year by the Data Processing Management Association (1969), and awarded the National Medal of Technology (1991).

CHAPTER 10

JOHN MAUCHLY AND J. PRESPER ECKERT

Respectively, born Aug. 30, 1907, Cincinnati, Ohio, U.S.—died Jan. 8, 1980, Ambler, Pa., U.S.; born April 9, 1919, Philadelphia, Pa., U.S.—died June 3, 1995, Bryn Mawr, Pa., U.S.

American engineers John William Mauchly and John Presper Eckert, Jr., were coinventors in 1946 of the Electronic Numerical Integrator and Computer (ENIAC). The ENIAC was a general-purpose electronic digital computer that many computer historians believe to have been the first of its kind, at least in the United States.

Mauchly received a doctorate in physics from Johns Hopkins University, Baltimore, Md., in 1932 and entered teaching as a professor of physics. Eventually his work led him into the design of electrical circuits that would aid in the performing of mathematical computations. During World War II he earned a certificate in electrical engineering at the Moore School of Electrical Engineering at the University of Pennsylvania, Philadelphia, and was offered a teaching position there.

Eckert had received his bachelor's degree (1941) and his master's degree (1943) at the Moore School, where as a graduate student he was one of Mauchly's lab instructors. Mauchly and Eckert were asked to devise ways to accelerate the recomputation of artillery firing tables for the U.S. Army. They accordingly proposed the construction of an electronic computer that would handle data in digital form. By 1946 they completed the ENIAC, a huge machine (containing more than 18,000 vacuum tubes) that in primitive form contained virtually all the circuitry used in present-day high-speed digital computers. The machine could be programmed to perform different kinds of calculations at high speed and in December 1945 solved its first problem—calculations for the hydrogen bomb. After its official unveiling in February 1946, the ENIAC was first used by the U.S. Army at its Aberdeen Proving Ground in Maryland in 1947 for ballistics tests.

That year the University of Pennsylvania ordered its employees to sign over all patent rights to work done on computers during the war. Mauchly and Eckert refused and resigned their positions in March 1946 to form their own computer-manufacturing firm, the Eckert-Mauchly Computer Corporation. In 1949 they announced the Binary Automatic Computer (BINAC), which stored data on magnetic tape instead of punched cards and was the

J. Presper Eckert (right) *and John Mauchly.* Alfred Eisenstaedt/Time & Life Pictures/Getty Images

first stored-program computer in the United States. The third computer after BINAC was UNIVAC I, specially designed to handle business data. Delivered in 1951 to the U.S. Census Bureau, UNIVAC found many uses in commerce and may be said to have started the computer boom.

In 1950, meanwhile, the Eckert-Mauchly company and all of its patents, including patents for ENIAC, had been acquired by Remington Rand Inc., which was merged in 1955 into the Sperry Rand Corp. (later Unisys Corp.). In 1967 Sperry Rand filed a lawsuit against Honeywell Inc. to protect its patents on electronic digital computers (based largely on its acquisition of the ENIAC patent). However, portions of the patent (which covered essentially all aspects of electronic digital computers) were ruled by the court to have derived from the Atanasoff-Berry Computer of the 1930s and from information imparted to Mauchly by John V. Atanasoff in the early 1940s. In 1973 Sperry Rand's patent claim was ruled invalid by a federal court. (Most historians, however, continue to give precedence to Eckert and Mauchly over Atanasoff because of the complexity and programmability inherent in ENIAC's design, as opposed to Atanasoff's limited-function machine.)

Eckert remained in executive positions after the acquisition by Remington Rand. He retired from Unisys in 1989. Between 1948 and 1966 he received 85 patents, mostly for electronic inventions. He was awarded the National Medal of Science in 1968.

Mauchly worked at Remington Rand as director of special projects until 1959, when he founded his own consulting firm, Mauchly Associates Inc. He served as president (1959–65) and chairman of the board (1965–69) of Mauchly Associates and also as president (1968–80) of Dynatrend Inc., another consulting firm that he founded.

CHAPTER 11

HOWARD AIKEN

Born March 9, 1900, Hoboken, N.J., U.S.—died March 14, 1973, St. Louis, Mo., U.S.

Howard Hathaway Aiken was an American mathematician who invented the Harvard Mark I, a forerunner of the modern electronic digital computer.

Aiken did engineering work while he attended the University of Wisconsin, Madison. After completing his doctorate at Harvard University in 1939, he remained there for a short period to teach before undertaking war work for the U.S. Navy Board of Ordnance.

With three other engineers—Clair D. Lake, B.M. Durfee, and F.E. Hamilton—Aiken began work in 1939 on an automatic calculating machine that could perform any selected sequence of five arithmetical operations (addition, subtraction, multiplication, division, and reference to previous results) without human intervention. The first such machine, the Mark I, was completed by Aiken and his partners in February 1944: 51 feet (15.3 metres) long and 8 feet (2.4 metres) high, it weighed 35 tons (31,500 kg) and contained about 500 miles (800 km) of wire and more than 3,000,000 connections. The Mark I was programmed to solve problems by means of a paper tape on which coded instructions were punched. Once so programmed, the calculator could be operated by persons with little training. The Mark I was used by the U.S. Navy for work in gunnery, ballistics, and design. Continuing his work, Aiken completed an improved all-electric Mark II in 1947. He also wrote numerous articles on electronics, switching theory, and data processing.

CHAPTER 12

WILLIAM SHOCKLEY

Born Feb. 13, 1910, London, Eng.—died Aug. 12, 1989, Palo Alto, Calif., U.S.

William Bradford Shockley was an American engineer and teacher. He was a cowinner (with John Bardeen and Walter H. Brattain) of the Nobel Prize for Physics in 1956 for the development of the transistor, a device that largely replaced the bulkier and less-efficient vacuum tube and ushered in the age of microminiature electronics.

Shockley was born in London to American parents, who moved to Palo Alto, Calif., when he was a small boy. He studied physics at the California Institute of Technology (B.S., 1932) and the Massachusetts Institute of Technology (Ph.D., 1936). He joined the technical staff of the Bell Telephone Laboratories in 1936 and there began experiments with semiconductors that ultimately led to the invention and development of the transistor. During World War II, he served as director of research for the Antisubmarine Warfare Operations Research Group of the U.S. Navy.

After the war, Shockley returned to Bell Labs as director of its research program on solid-state physics. Working with Bardeen and Brattain, he resumed his attempts to use semiconductors as amplifiers and controllers of electronic signals. The three men invented the point-contact transistor in 1947 and a more effective device, the junction transistor, in 1948.

Shockley was deputy director of the Weapons Systems Evaluation Group of the Department of Defense in

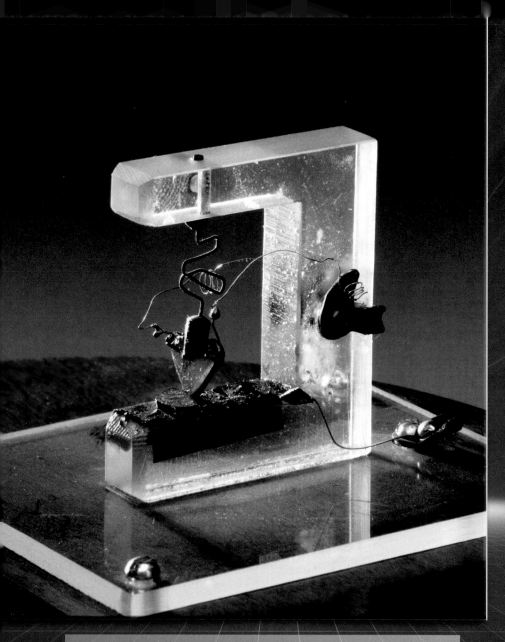

William Shockley, together with John Bardeen and Walter H. Brattain, won the Nobel Prize for Physics for the development of the transistor (a replica is shown here). SSPL via Getty Images

1954–55. He joined Beckman Instruments Inc. to establish the Shockley Semiconductor Laboratory in 1956 in Palo Alto to produce high-speed transistors. Within a year a group of eight dissatisfied engineers resigned en masse to join with Fairchild Camera and Instrument Corporation to establish Fairchild Semiconductor Corporation in nearby Santa Clara. Engineers from Fairchild went on to coinvent the integrated circuit in 1958, and that company helped to spark an electronics boom that transformed the area around Palo Alto into today's Silicon Valley.

In 1958 Shockley became lecturer at Stanford University in Palo Alto. Then in 1963 he became the first Poniatoff professor of engineering science there (emeritus, 1974). He wrote *Electrons and Holes in Semiconductors* (1950).

During the late 1960s, Shockley became a figure of some controversy because of his widely debated views on the intellectual differences between races. He held that standardized intelligence tests reflect a genetic factor in intellectual capacity and that tests for IQ (intelligence quotient) reveal that blacks are inferior to whites. He further concluded that the higher rate of reproduction among blacks had a retrogressive effect on evolution.

CHAPTER 13

ALAN TURING

Born June 23, 1912, London, Eng.—died June 7, 1954, Wilmslow, Cheshire, Eng.

Alan Mathison Turing was a British mathematician and logician who made major contributions to mathematics, cryptanalysis, logic, philosophy, and biology and to the new areas later named computer science, cognitive science, artificial intelligence, and artificial life.

The son of a British member of the Indian civil service, Turing entered King's College, University of Cambridge, to study mathematics in 1931. After graduating in 1934, Turing was elected to a fellowship at King's College in recognition of his research in probability theory. In 1936 Turing's seminal paper "On Computable Numbers, with an Application to the *Entscheidungsproblem* [Decision Problem]" was recommended for publication by the American mathematician-logician Alonzo Church. The *Entscheidungsproblem* seeks an effective method for deciding which mathematical statements are provable within a given formal mathematical system and which are not. Both Turing and Church had independently shown that in general this problem has no solution, thus proving that no consistent formal system of arithmetic is decidable. Later in 1936, Turing moved to Princeton University to study for a Ph.D. in mathematical logic under Church's direction (completed in 1938).

In the course of his proof, Turing had introduced the notion of an abstract computer that is now known as the Turing machine. Not actually a machine, it was an idealized mathematical model that reduced the logical structure of any computing device to its essentials. It consisted of an infinitely extensible tape, a tape head that was capable of performing various operations on the tape, and a modifiable control mechanism in the head that could store instructions. As envisaged by Turing, the machine performed its functions in a sequence of discrete steps. Turing's extrapolation of these essential features of information processing was instrumental in the development of modern digital computers, which share his basic scheme of an input/output device (tape and tape reader), central processing unit (CPU, or control mechanism), and stored memory.

In the summer of 1938 Turing returned from the United States to his fellowship at King's College. At the outbreak of hostilities with Germany in September 1939, he joined the wartime headquarters of the Government Code and Cypher School at Bletchley Park, Buckinghamshire. There Turing and others designed a code-breaking machine known as the Bombe to break the Enigma code used by the German military for their radio communications. By early 1942 the Bletchley Park cryptanalysts were decoding about 39,000 intercepted messages each month, which rose subsequently to more than 84,000 per month. At the end of the war, Turing was made an officer of the Order of the British Empire for his code-breaking work.

In 1945, the war being over, Turing was recruited to the National Physical Laboratory (NPL) in London to design and develop an electronic computer. His design for the Automatic Computing Engine (ACE) was the first relatively complete specification of an electronic stored-program general-purpose digital computer. Had

A version of the German cipher machine, Enigma. Bletchley Park Trust/
SSPL via Getty Images

Turing's ACE been built as planned, it would have had
considerably more memory than any of the other early
computers, as well as being faster. However, his colleagues at NPL thought the engineering too difficult
to attempt, and a much simpler machine was built, the
Pilot Model ACE.

ULTRA WINS THE WAR

Ultra was an Allied intelligence project during World War II that tapped the very highest level of encrypted communications of the German armed forces, as well as those of the Italian and Japanese armed forces, and thus contributed to the Allied victory. At Bletchley Park, a British government establishment located north of London, a small group of code breakers developed techniques for decrypting intercepted messages that had been coded by German operators using electrical cipher machines, the most important of which were the Enigma and, later in the war, the sophisticated Tunny machine. The flood of high-grade military intelligence produced by Bletchley Park was code-named Ultra (from "Top Secret Ultra"). According to some experts, Ultra may have hastened Germany's defeat by as much as two years.

Every day the German military transmitted thousands of coded messages, ranging from orders signed by Adolf Hitler and detailed situation reports prepared by generals at the front line down through weather reports and supply ship inventories. Much of this information ended up in Allied hands, often within hours of being transmitted. The actual texts of the deciphered messages—the "raw decrypts"—rarely left Bletchley Park. Instead, analysts there sifted the decrypts and prepared intelligence reports that carefully concealed the true source of the information.

The Enigma machine, looking rather like a typewriter, was battery-powered and highly portable. In addition to a keyboard, the device had a lamp board consisting of 26 stenciled letters, each with a small lightbulb behind it. As a cipher clerk typed a message on the keyboard in plain German, letters were illuminated one by one on the lamp board. An assistant recorded the letters by hand to form the enciphered message, which was then transmitted in Morse Code.

Each bulb in the lamp board was electrically connected to a letter on the keyboard, but the wiring passed via a number of rotating wheels, with the result that the connections were always changing as the wheels moved. Thus, typing the same letter at the keyboard, such as AAAA..., would produce a stream of changing letters at the lamp board, such as WMEV.... It was this ever-changing pattern of connections that made Enigma extremely hard to break.

The earliest success against the German military Enigma was by the Polish Cipher Bureau. In the winter of 1932–33, Polish mathematician Marian Rejewski deduced the pattern of wiring inside the three rotating wheels of the Enigma machine. Before an Enigma operator began enciphering a message, he set Enigma's wheels to various starting positions that were also known to the intended recipient. In a major breakthrough, Rejewski invented a method for finding out the positions in which the wheels had started at the beginning of the message. In consequence, Poland was able to read encrypted German messages from 1933 to 1939. In the summer of 1939 Poland turned over everything to Britain and France. In May 1940, however, a radical change to the Enigma system eliminated the loophole that Rejewski had exploited to discover the starting positions of the wheels.

New methods developed at Bletchley Park during 1940 enabled code breakers there to continue to decipher German air force and army communications. However, German naval messages—including the all-important traffic to and from U-boats in the North Atlantic—remained cloaked. (The Poles too had had little success against naval Enigma.) U-boats were sinking such a large number of merchant ships taking food, munitions, and oil to Britain from North America that by 1941 some analysts were predicting that the sinkings would tip Britain into starvation within a few months. In June 1941 British mathematician Alan M. Turing and his group at Bletchley finally succeeded in breaking into the daily communications of the U-boats. Decoded messages revealed the positions of the submarines, enabling ships to avoid contact. Great care was always exercised to conceal the fact that Bletchley had deciphered these messages. For instance, British intelligence leaked false information hinting at revolutionary new developments in long-range radar.

Turing was responsible for another major development in breaking Enigma. In March 1940, Turing's first Bombe, a code-breaking machine, was installed at Bletchley Park. This complex machine consisted of approximately 100 rotating drums, 10 miles of wire, and about 1 million soldered connections. The Bombe searched through different possible positions of Enigma's internal wheels, looking for a pattern of keyboard-to-lamp board connections that would turn coded letters into plain German. The method depended on human instinct, though; to initiate the process, a code breaker had to guess a few words in the message (these guessed words were called a crib). The war on Enigma was transformed by the high-speed Bombes, and the production of Ultra grew as more of them were installed in Britain and the United States.

In 1940 the Germans produced a state-of-the-art 12-wheel cipher machine, code-named Tunny by the British. Only one operator was necessary—unlike Enigma, which typically involved three (a typist, a transcriber, and a radio operator). The Tunny operator simply typed in plain German at the keyboard, and the rest of the process was automated. Under normal operating conditions, neither the sender nor the receiver ever saw the coded message.

Tunny began operational use in June 1941, and by July 1942 Bletchley Park was in a position to read the messages regularly—thanks, in particular, to a series of breakthroughs by British mathematician William Tutte. It was soon discovered that Tunny, unlike Enigma, carried only the highest grade of intelligence—messages between the German army's high command and the generals in the field. Tunny decrypts provided detailed knowledge of German strategy, most notably the counterpreparations for the anticipated Allied invasion of northern France in 1944.

Turing's anti-Enigma Bombe was of no use against Tunny; to crack the high volumes of messages, different machines were developed. The first Tunny-breaking machine (called Heath Robinson, after British cartoonist William Heath Robinson, known for drawing absurdly ingenious contrivances) was installed at Bletchley in 1943, but it was never entirely satisfactory. British engineer Thomas Flowers took a different tack and built an electronic computer for Tunny breaking. His Colossus, the world's first large-scale programmable electronic computer, was constructed in London and installed at Bletchley in January 1944. By the end of the war, 10 models operated round-the-clock for Tunny breaking. The full nature and scope of Bletchley's attack on Tunny was not revealed until 2000, when the British government declassified a 500-page document written in 1945, "General Report on Tunny with Emphasis on Statistical Methods."

In the end, NPL lost the race to build the world's first working electronic stored-program digital computer—an honour that went to the Royal Society Computing Machine Laboratory at the University of Manchester in June 1948. Discouraged by the delays at NPL, Turing took up the deputy directorship of the Computing Machine Laboratory in that year (there was no director). His earlier theoretical concept of a universal Turing machine had been a fundamental influence on the Manchester computer project from its inception. Turing's principal practical contribution after his arrival at Manchester was to design the programming system of the Ferranti Mark I, the world's first commercially available electronic digital computer.

Though he was elected a fellow of the Royal Society in March 1951, Turing's life was about to suffer a major reversal. In March 1952 he was prosecuted for homosexuality, then a crime in Britain, and sentenced to 12 months of hormone "therapy"—a treatment that he seems to have borne with amused fortitude. Judged a security risk by the British government, Turing lost his security clearance and his access to ongoing government work with codes and computers. He spent the rest of his short career at the University of Manchester, where he was appointed to a specially created readership in the theory of computing in May 1953.

From 1951 Turing had been working on what is now known as artificial life. He wrote "The Chemical Basis of Morphogenesis," which described some of his research on the development of pattern and form in living organisms, and he used the Ferranti Mark I computer to model chemical mechanisms by which genes could control the development of anatomical structure in plants and animals. In the midst of this groundbreaking work, Turing was discovered dead in his bed, poisoned by cyanide. A homemade apparatus for silver-plating teaspoons, which included a tank of cyanide, was found in the room next to his bedroom. The official verdict was suicide, but no motive was ever discovered.

CHAPTER 14

WILLIAM HEWLETT AND DAVID PACKARD

Respectively, born May 20, 1913, Ann Arbor, Mich., U.S.—died Jan. 12, 2001, Palo Alto, Calif., U.S.; born Sept. 7, 1912, Pueblo, Colo., U.S.—died March 26, 1996, Stanford, Calif., U.S.

American engineers and businessmen William Redington Hewlett and David Packard were the cofounders of the Hewlett-Packard Company (HP), an electronics and computer giant credited with pioneering California's Silicon Valley and thus the computer age.

Hewlett's interest in science and electronics began when he was a child, and in 1930 he began studying engineering at Stanford University. It was there that he met Packard, and the two became lifelong friends. After graduation in 1934, Hewlett earned a master's degree at the Massachusetts Institute of Technology in 1936 and then returned to Stanford for further study. Packard also received his B.A. from Stanford in 1934. He then went to work for the General Electric Company in Schenectady, N.Y. In 1938 he, like Hewlett, returned to Stanford, where he earned the degree of electrical engineer.

On Jan. 1, 1939, at the suggestion of engineering professor Frederick Terman and with start-up funds of $538, Hewlett and Packard set up a small electronics business in a rented garage in Palo Alto. That garage was later (1989) designated a California historical landmark. One of HP's products, an audio oscillator, brought the company its first success when Walt Disney Productions purchased eight of the devices to test sound equipment

To test sound equipment for its animated film Fantasia, *Walt Disney Productions purchased audio oscillators from Hewlett-Packard, giving the company its first success.* © SuperStock

for the animated film *Fantasia* (1940). During World War II the company developed products for military applications that were important enough to merit Packard a draft exemption, while Hewlett served in the Army Signal Corps.

Following his wartime service, Hewlett returned to HP in 1947 and was made a vice president, and in 1964 he became president, a position he retained until 1977. Hewlett also served as HP's chief executive officer (CEO) from 1969 to 1978, chairman of the executive committee from 1977 to 1983, vice chairman of the board from 1983 to 1987, and director emeritus from 1987 until his death. Packard, meanwhile, served as HP's president from 1947 to 1964, CEO from 1964 to 1968, and chairman of the board from 1964 to 1968 and from 1972 to 1993. Although semiretired during the 1980s, he returned in 1991 to steer the company through a financial slump.

The company, in which Packard proved to be an expert administrator and Hewlett provided many technical innovations, grew into the world's largest producer of electronic testing and measurement devices. In 1968 HP produced the first desktop scientific calculator. The pocket scientific calculator followed in 1972, rendering slide rules largely obsolete. HP became even better known in 1984 with its laser-jet printer. The company eventually became the second largest computer maker, and Hewlett and Packard became two of the wealthiest Americans.

Early in the company's history, the two founders endorsed formal management procedures, and HP was one of the first corporations to use the "management by objective" approach. They also created an informal workplace, encouraging the use of first names among employees, even for themselves. Packard and Hewlett were also known for "management by walking around," visiting as many departments as possible without appointments or scheduled meetings and talking with line workers as often as with managers to better understand how the company was operating. HP became one of the first businesses in the United States to endorse the idea that employees, customers, and the community have as valid an interest in company performance as do shareholders. As a result, it consistently ranked among the best places to work for women and minorities. It also became one of the leading contributors to charitable organizations, donating as much as 4.4 percent of its pretax profits. In 1966 Hewlett and his first wife, Flora, established the William and Flora Hewlett Foundation, which made bequests to numerous environmental, arts, educational, and social causes.

From 1968 to 1971 Packard served as deputy secretary of defense, and in the 1970s and '80s he was a prominent adviser to the U.S. president on defense procurement and management. He was also a major contributor to conservative institutions and causes. Packard received numerous awards, including the Presidential Medal of Freedom in 1988. In 1985 Hewlett was honoured with the National Medal of Science, the highest scientific award in the United States.

CHAPTER 15

MAURICE WILKES

Born June 26, 1913, Dudley, Staffordshire, Eng.—died Nov. 29, 2010, Cambridge, Cambridgeshire, Eng.

Maurice Vincent Wilkes was a British computer science pioneer who in 1946–49 helped build the Electronic Delay Storage Automatic Calculator (EDSAC), the first full-size stored-program computer, and invented microprogramming.

Wilkes became interested in electronics as a boy and studied that subject in his spare time while working toward a degree in mathematics (1934) at St. John's College, Cambridge. He then did graduate work at the university's Cavendish Laboratory (M.A., 1936; Ph.D., 1937). His interest in computing was sparked in 1936 by a lecture by English physicist and computer pioneer Douglas Hartree. In 1937 the Mathematical Laboratory, which used mechanical computers for scientific projects, was founded at Cambridge. Wilkes was appointed university demonstrator there and was the Mathematical Laboratory's only staff member.

During World War II Wilkes left Cambridge to work elsewhere on the development of radar and a bomb-aiming system for aircraft. He returned to the Mathematical Laboratory as director in 1945.

In May 1946 Wilkes read American mathematician John von Neumann's paper *First Draft of a Report on the EDVAC* (1945), which described the planned Electronic Discrete Variable Automatic Computer (EDVAC), in which both the data and the programs that would manipulate the data would be stored within EDVAC's memory. This stored-program computer was an advance upon previous machines such as the Electronic Numerical Integrator and Computer (ENIAC), in which the program instructions were determined by the wiring of the machine. Wilkes was convinced by von Neumann's paper that all future computers would be stored-program machines. Later in 1946 Wilkes attended a summer school on the design of electronic computers at the University of Pennsylvania in Philadelphia. On the voyage home to England, he began designing EDSAC. Work began on EDSAC in 1946, and it became operational in May 1949.

Maurice Wilkes developed EDSAC (Electronic Delay Storage Automatic Calculator), the first full-scale stored-program computer, to learn more about computer programming issues. SSPL via Getty Images

Wilkes built EDSAC chiefly to study computer programming issues, which he realized would become as important as the hardware details. Based on his experience in writing programs for EDSAC, he cowrote with David J. Wheeler and Stanley Gill *The Preparation of Programs for an Electronic Digital Computer* (1951), the first book on computer programming. EDSAC was used for research in physics, astronomy, and meteorology, and biochemist John Kendrew used EDSAC to determine the three-dimensional structure of the muscle protein myoglobin, for which he won the Nobel Prize for Chemistry in 1962.

In 1951 Wilkes wrote the first paper that described microprogramming, a term that he invented to describe how the stored program could be used to run the operations of the computer itself. The idea of microprogramming was first tested in 1957 on a small machine called EDSAC 1.5. The first full-size microprogrammed computer was EDSAC 2, which became operational in 1958. The successful example of EDSAC 2 inspired IBM to make its family of versatile System/360 model computers microprogrammed.

Wilkes became a professor of computer technology at Cambridge in 1965. That year he also wrote the first paper on cache memory (which he called "slave memory"), an extension of the computer's main memory in which frequently used instructions and data are stored for quicker processing. In 1975 he wrote a paper describing client-server architecture computing, which was implemented in 1980 with the Cambridge Ring network. He retired from Cambridge in 1980 and moved to the United States, where he was a senior consulting engineer at the American manufacturer Digital Equipment Corporation in Maynard, Mass., from 1980 to 1986. He was also an adjunct professor of electrical engineering and computer science at the Massachusetts Institute of Technology from 1981 to 1985. He returned to England, and from 1986 to 2002 he was an adviser and consultant at the Olivetti and Oracle Research Laboratory (later AT&T Laboratories) in Cambridge.

Wilkes was elected a fellow of the Royal Society in 1956. He won the A.M. Turing Award in 1967 and the Kyoto Prize in 1992. In 1985 he published an autobiography, *Memoirs of a Computer Pioneer*. Wilkes was knighted in 2000.

CHAPTER 16

CLAUDE SHANNON

Born April 30, 1916, Petoskey, Mich., U.S.—died Feb. 24, 2001, Medford, Mass., U.S.

Claude Elwood Shannon was an American mathematician and electrical engineer who laid the theoretical foundations for digital circuits and information theory, a mathematical communication model.

After graduating from the University of Michigan in 1936 with bachelor's degrees in mathematics and electrical engineering, Shannon obtained a research assistant's position at the Massachusetts Institute of Technology (MIT). There, among other duties, he worked with the noted researcher Vannevar Bush, helping to set up differential equations on Bush's Differential Analyzer. A summer internship at American Telephone and Telegraph's Bell Laboratories in New York City in 1937 inspired much of Shannon's subsequent research interests. In 1940 he earned both a master's degree in electrical engineering and a Ph.D. in mathematics from MIT. He joined the mathematics department at Bell Labs in 1941, where he first contributed to work on antiaircraft missile control systems. He remained affiliated with Bell Labs until 1972. Shannon became a visiting professor at MIT in 1956, a permanent member of the faculty in 1958, and professor emeritus in 1978.

Shannon's master's thesis, "A Symbolic Analysis of Relay and Switching Circuits" (1940), used Boolean algebra to establish the theoretical underpinnings of digital circuits. Because digital circuits are fundamental to the

Claude Shannon. Keystone/Hulton Archive/Getty Images

operation of modern computers and telecommunications equipment, this dissertation was called one of the most significant master's theses of the 20th century. In contrast, his doctoral thesis, "An Algebra for Theoretical Genetics" (1940), was not as influential.

In 1948 Shannon published "A Mathematical Theory of Communication," which built on the foundations of other researchers at Bell Labs such as Harry Nyquist and R.V.L. Hartley. Shannon's paper, however, went far beyond the earlier work. It established the basic results of information theory in such a complete form that his framework and terminology are still used. (The paper appears to contain the first published use of the term *bit* to designate a single binary digit.)

An important step taken by Shannon was to separate the technical problem of delivering a message from the problem of understanding what a message means. This step permitted engineers to focus on the message delivery system. Shannon concentrated on two key questions in his 1948 paper: determining the most efficient encoding of a message using a given alphabet in a noiseless environment, and understanding what additional steps need to be taken in the presence of noise.

Shannon solved these problems successfully for a very abstract (hence widely applicable) model of a communications system that includes both discrete (digital) and continuous (analog) systems. In particular, he developed a measure of the efficiency of a communications system, called the entropy (analogous to the thermodynamic concept of entropy, which measures the amount of disorder in physical systems), that is computed on the basis of the statistical properties of the message source.

Shannon's formulation of information theory was an immediate success with communications engineers and continues to prove useful. It also inspired many attempts to apply information theory in other areas, such as cognition, biology, linguistics, psychology, economics, and physics. In fact, there was so much enthusiasm in this direction that in 1956 Shannon wrote a paper, "The Bandwagon," to moderate some overenthusiastic proponents.

Renowned for his eclectic interests and capabilities—including such activities as juggling while riding a unicycle down the halls of Bell Labs—Shannon produced many provocative and influential articles on information theory, cryptography, and chess-playing computers, as well as designing various mechanical devices.

CHAPTER 17

TOM KILBURN

Born Aug. 11, 1921, Dewsbury, Yorkshire, Eng.—died Jan. 17, 2001, Manchester, Eng.

British engineer and coinventor of the first working computer memory. Kilburn also designed and built the first stored-program computer and led a team that produced a succession of pioneering computers over the next 25 years.

In 1942 Kilburn graduated from the University of Cambridge with a degree in mathematics. He immediately converted, however, to electronics research when he was recruited to join Frederic Williams's wartime radar group at the Telecommunications Research Establishment (TRE). In December 1946 Williams left TRE to become a professor at the University of Manchester, and Kilburn accompanied him to help develop an electronic storage system for electronic computers. They devised a storage device—later known as the Williams tube—based on cathode-ray tubes. A working model was completed late in 1947, and by June 1948 they had incorporated it in a small electronic computer that they built to prove the device's effectiveness. The computer was called the Small Scale Experimental Machine (SSEM) or just "Baby." It was the world's first working stored-program computer, and the Williams tube became one of the two standard methods of storage used by computers worldwide until the advent of magnetic-core storage in the mid-1950s. By April 1949 the SSEM had developed into a full-sized machine, and by October 1949 secondary storage had been added (using a magnetic drum). This machine, the Manchester Mark I, was the prototype for the Ferranti Mark I, manufactured by Ferranti Ltd.

From 1951 Kilburn formally led the computer group within Williams's electrical engineering department. In 1953 the group completed an experimental computer using transistors instead of vacuum tubes. In 1954 the group completed MEG, which provided floating-point arithmetic (calculations using exponential notation—e.g., 3.27 × 10^{17}) and was manufactured by Ferranti as the Mercury beginning in 1957.

In 1956 Kilburn started his most ambitious project, MUSE, renamed Atlas when Ferranti joined the project in 1959. In parallel with two similar projects in the United States (LARC and Stretch) but largely independent of them, Atlas made the massive jump from running one program at a time to multiprogramming. With multiprogramming a computer can "interleave" several programs, allocating various computer resources (memory, storage, input, and output) to each program through an operating system. Atlas was also the first computer to employ a technique, now known as virtual memory or virtual storage, of using some slower external memory (such as magnetic drums) as though it were an extension of the computer's faster internal memory. Operational by 1962, Atlas was probably the most sophisticated computer of its time.

In 1964 Kilburn created the first department of computer science in the United Kingdom. In 1966 he started his last computer project, MU5. Operational by 1972, MU5 pioneered an architecture geared to the requirements of high-level languages (languages with more humanlike syntax).

Kilburn was made a professor in 1960 and was elected a fellow of the Royal Society in 1965. He retired in 1981.

CHAPTER 18

ALAN PERLIS

Born April 1, 1922, Pittsburgh, Pa., U.S.—died Feb. 7, 1990, New Haven, Conn., U.S.

Alan Jay Perlis was an American mathematician and computer scientist. He was the first winner, in 1966, of the A.M. Turing Award, given by the Association of Computing Machinery (ACM) and recognized internationally as the highest honour in computer science. In particular, Perlis was cited for "his influence in the area of advanced programming techniques and compiler construction." Perlis was one of the most important individuals in establishing computer science as a distinct academic field.

In 1943 Perlis earned a bachelor's degree in chemistry from the Carnegie Institute of Technology (now Carnegie Mellon University). During World War II, he served in the U.S. Army Air Forces in Europe. Following the war Perlis earned a master's degree (1949) and a doctorate (1950) in mathematics from the Massachusetts Institute of Technology, where he worked on Whirlwind, the first real-time computer.

In 1952 Perlis became a mathematics professor and the first director of the computing laboratory at Purdue University. Perlis returned to the Carnegie Institute as director of the school's computation centre (1956–60), chairman of the mathematics department (1960–64), and chairman of the computer science department (1965–71). The ACM in 1957 appointed Perlis chairman of a committee to establish a higher-level computer programming language. ALGOL, as the new language was later named, led to Pascal, which remains a widely used scientific programming language.

In 1971 Perlis became the Eugene Higgins Professor of Computer Science at Yale University, where he served as chair of the computer science department (1976–80) except for during the 1977–78 academic year, when he was at the California Institute of Technology. He remained at Yale for the rest of his life.

In 1982 Perlis wrote "Epigrams on Programming" for the *SIGPLAN Notices* of the ACM, which described in simple epigrams his philosophy of computer programming. Some of the Zen-like aphorisms include:

- Optimization hinders evolution.
- To understand a program you must become both the machine and the program.
- A year spent in artificial intelligence is enough to make one believe in God.

Perlis was a member of the American Academy of Arts and Sciences and the U.S. National Academy of Engineering. He was the first editor (1958–62) of *Communications of the ACM* and president of the ACM from 1962 to 1964.

CHAPTER 19

SEYMOUR CRAY

Born Sept. 28, 1925, Chippewa Falls, Wis., U.S.—died Oct. 5, 1996, Colorado Springs, Colo., U.S.

Seymour Roger Cray was an American electronics engineer who was the preeminent designer of the large, high-speed computers known as supercomputers.

Cray graduated from the University of Minnesota in 1950 with a bachelor's degree in electrical engineering. He began his career with a computer company called Engineering Research Associates (ERA) in 1951. When ERA was taken over by Remington Rand Inc. (which later merged with other companies to become Unisys Corporation), Cray worked on UNIVAC I, a landmark first-generation electronic digital computer that became the first commercially available computer. In 1957 he left with ERA's founder, William Norris, to start Control Data Corporation (CDC). By that time the UNIVAC line of computers and IBM had divided up most of the market for business computers, and, rather than challenge their extensive sales and support structures, CDC sought to capture the small but lucrative market for fast scientific computers. The Cray-designed CDC 1604 was one of the first computers to replace vacuum tubes with transistors and was quite popular in scientific laboratories. In 1964 Cray's CDC 6600 was the fastest computer on Earth; it could execute three million floating-point operations per second (FLOPS), and the term *supercomputer* was soon coined to describe it.

Cray left CDC to start Cray Research Inc. in 1972 and moved on again in 1981 and in 1989. Each time he moved on, his former company continued producing supercomputers based on his designs. Cray was deeply involved in every aspect of creating the computers that his companies built. In particular, he was a genius at the dense packaging of the electronic components that make up a computer. By clever design he cut the distances signals had to travel, thereby speeding up the machines. He always strove to create the fastest possible computer for the scientific market, programmed in the scientific programming language of choice (FORTRAN), and optimized the machines for demanding scientific applications (e.g., differential equations, matrix manipulations, fluid dynamics, seismic analysis, and linear programming).

Among Cray's pioneering achievements was the Cray-1, introduced in 1976, which was the first successful implementation of vector processing (meaning it could operate on pairs of lists of numbers rather than on mere pairs of numbers). The Cray-1 could perform 240 million FLOPS. It was used for large-scale scientific applications, such as simulating complex physical phenomena, and was sold to government and university laboratories.

Cray resigned as chairman of his growing firm in 1981 and became an independent contractor to the company, designing ever-faster machines at his laboratory in Chippewa Falls. He was one of the pioneers of dividing complex computations among multiple processors, a design known as "multiprocessing." One of the first machines to use multiprocessing was the Cray X-MP, introduced in 1982, which linked two Cray-1 computers in parallel to triple their individual performance. In 1985 the Cray-2, a four-processor computer, became the first machine to exceed one billion FLOPS. The Cray Y-MP, introduced in 1988, was capable of 2.67 billion FLOPS.

In 1989 Cray founded the Cray Computer Corporation. However, as microprocessor technology advanced and the demand for supercomputers fell in the post-Cold War era, Cray Computers filed for bankruptcy in 1995. Undaunted, however, Cray opened another company, SRC Computer Inc., in August 1996, only two months before his death as a result of injuries sustained in a car crash.

CHAPTER 20

DOUGLAS ENGELBART

Born Jan. 30, 1925, near Portland, Ore., U.S.

Douglas Engelbart is an American inventor whose work beginning in the 1950s led to his patent for the computer mouse, the development of the basic graphical user interface, and groupware. Engelbart won the 1997 A.M. Turing Award, the highest honour in computer science, for his "inspiring vision of the future of interactive computing and the invention of key technologies to help realize this vision."

Engelbart grew up on a farm near Portland. Following two years of enlisted service as a radar technician for the U.S. Navy in World War II, he completed a bachelor's degree in electrical engineering at Oregon State University in 1948. He soon became dissatisfied with his electrical engineering job at the Ames Research Center, located at Moffett Field, California, and in December 1950 had the inspiration that would drive the rest of his professional life.

Engelbart's dream was to use computers to connect individuals in a network that would allow them to share and update information in "real time." He combined this idea of collaborative software, or groupware, with his experience interpreting radar displays and with ideas he gleaned from an *Atlantic Monthly* article by Vannevar Bush, "As We May Think," to envision networked computers employing a graphical user interface. After receiving a doctorate in electrical engineering from the University of California at Berkeley in 1955, he stayed on as an acting assistant professor for a year before accepting a position with the Stanford Research Institute (SRI) in Stanford, Calif.

In 1963 Engelbart was given funding by SRI to start his own research laboratory, the Augmentation Research Center, where he worked on inventing and perfecting various devices—such as the computer mouse, the multiple window display, and hypermedia (the linking of texts, images, video, and sound files within a single document)—for inputting, manipulating, and displaying data. Together with a colleague at SRI, William English, he eventually perfected a variety of input devices—including joysticks, light pens, and track balls—that are now common. Prior to Engelbart's inventions, laborious and error-prone keypunch cards or manually set electronic switches were necessary to control computers, and data had to be printed before it could be viewed. His work made it possible for ordinary people to use computers.

Early in 1967 Engelbart's laboratory became the second site on the Advanced Research Projects Agency Network (ARPANET), the primary precursor to the Internet. On Dec. 9, 1968, at a computer conference in San Francisco, Engelbart demonstrated a working real-time collaborative computer system known as NLS (oNLine System). Using NLS, he and English (back at Stanford) worked on a shared document in one window (using keyboard and mouse input devices) while at the same time conducting the world's first public computer video conference in another window. Engelbart continued his research, building increasingly sophisticated input and display devices and improving the graphical user interface, but because of budget cuts at SRI most of his research staff migrated to other institutions such as Xerox Corporation's Palo Alto Research Center in Palo Alto, Calif.

Here, computer interface pioneer Douglas Engelbart holds a video conference on the right side of the computer screen while working on a document with a remote collaborator on the left side of the screen during a 1968 computer conference in San Francisco, Calif. Courtesy of the Bootstrap Institute

In 1977 SRI sold Engelbart's NLS groupware system to Tymshare, Incorporated, a telephone networking company that renamed it Augment and sought to make it into a commercially viable office automation system. As the last remaining member of his research laboratory, and with SRI showing no further interest in his work, Engelbart joined Tymshare. In 1984 Tymshare was acquired by the McDonnell Douglas Corporation, where Engelbart worked on information systems. In 1989 he founded the Bootstrap Institute, a research and consulting firm. Over the following decade he finally began to receive recognition for his innovations.

MARVIN MINSKY

Born Aug. 9, 1927, New York, N.Y., U.S.

American mathematician and computer scientist Marvin Minsky is one of the most famous practitioners of the science of artificial intelligence (AI). Minsky won the 1969 A.M. Turing Award, the most prestigious award in computer science, for his pioneering work in AI.

In 1946, following service in the U.S. Navy from 1944 to 1945, Minsky enrolled at Harvard University to explore his many intellectual interests. After completing research in physics, neurophysiology, and psychology, Minsky graduated with honours in mathematics in 1950. In 1951 he entered Princeton University, and in that same year he built the first neural network simulator. In 1954, with a doctorate in mathematics from Princeton, Minsky returned to Harvard as a member of the prestigious Society of Fellows. He invented the confocal scanning microscope in 1955.

In 1957 Minsky moved to the Massachusetts Institute of Technology (MIT) to pursue his interest in using computers to model and understand human thought. Among others interested in AI was John McCarthy, an MIT professor of electrical engineering who had developed the LISP computer programming language and contributed to the development of time-sharing computer systems (systems in which multiple users interact with a single mainframe computer). In 1959 Minsky and McCarthy cofounded what became the MIT AI Laboratory. It quickly became one of the preeminent research centres and training grounds for the nascent field of AI. Minsky remained at MIT for the rest of his career, becoming Donner Professor of Science in 1974 and Toshiba Professor of Media Arts and Sciences at the MIT Media Laboratory in 1990.

Minsky defined AI as "the science of making machines do things that would require intelligence if done by men." Despite some early successes, AI researchers found it increasingly difficult to capture the external world in the cold, hard syntax of even the most powerful computer programming languages. In 1975 Minsky developed the concept of "frames" to identify precisely the general information that must be programmed into a computer before considering specific directions. For example, if a system had to navigate through a series of rooms connected by doors, Minsky suggested that the frame would need to articulate the associated range of possibilities for doors—in other words, all the commonsense knowledge that a child brings to bear when confronting a door: that the door may swing either way on a hinge, that the door can open and close, and that a door knob may have to be turned before pushing or pulling to open the door. Frames proved to be a rich concept among AI researchers, but applying it to highly complex situations has proved difficult.

Based on his experiences with frames and developmental child psychology, Minsky wrote *The Society of Mind* (1987), in which he presented his view of the mind as composed of individual agents performing basic functions, such as balance, movement, and comparison. However, critics contend that the "society of mind" idea is most accessible to laypeople and barely useful to AI researchers.

CHAPTER 22

ROBERT NOYCE

Born Dec. 12, 1927, Burlington, Iowa, U.S.—died June 3, 1990, Austin, Tex., U.S.

Robert Norton Noyce, an American engineer, was coinventor of the integrated circuit, a system of interconnected transistors on a single silicon microchip.

In 1939 the Noyce family moved to Grinnell, Iowa, where the father had accepted a position as a Congregational minister and where his son Robert began to demonstrate the traits of an inventor and tinkerer. Noyce majored in physics at Grinnell College (B.A., 1949) and earned a doctorate in solid state physics from the Massachusetts Institute of Technology (MIT; Ph.D., 1953), for a dissertation related to the technology he found most fascinating, the transistor.

Developed at Bell Laboratories in 1947, the transistor had figured in Noyce's imagination since he saw an early one in a college physics class. In 1956, while working for Philco Corporation, Noyce met William Shockley, one of the transistor's Nobel Prize–winning inventors. Shockley was recruiting researchers for Shockley Semiconductor Laboratory, a company that he had started in Palo Alto, Calif., to produce high-speed transistors. Noyce jumped at the opportunity, renting a house in Palo Alto even before his official job interview.

By early 1957, however, engineers at the new company had rebelled and attempted to force Shockley out of his management position, arguing that his poor management delayed production and adversely affected morale. Noyce and seven colleagues, among them Gordon Moore, resigned after failing to remove Shockley. With Noyce as their leader, the group—labeled the "traitorous eight" by Shockley—successfully negotiated with the Fairchild Camera and Instrument Company to form a new company, Fairchild Semiconductor Corporation, located in Santa Clara.

In 1958 Jean Hoerni, another Fairchild Semiconductor founder, engineered a process to place a layer of silicon oxide on top of transistors, sealing out dirt, dust, and other contaminants. For Noyce, Hoerni's process made a fundamental innovation possible. At that time, Fairchild produced transistors and other elements on large silicon wafers, cut the components out of the wafer, and later connected individual components with wires. However, as the number of connections increased, it became progressively more difficult to solder in ever smaller spaces. Noyce realized that rather than cutting the wafer apart, he could manufacture an entire circuit—complete with transistors, resistors, and other elements—on a single silicon wafer, the integrated circuit (IC). In this sense, Noyce and coinventor Jack Kilby, who was working at Texas Instruments Incorporated, thought along similar lines. They both saw the importance of the wafer, and each of their companies received patents on various aspects of IC design and manufacture. But Noyce saw further. Noyce saw that the solution to the problem of connecting the components was to evaporate lines of conductive metal (the "wires") directly onto the silicon wafer's surface, a technique known as the planar process. Kilby and Noyce share credit for independently inventing the integrated circuit. However, after much litigation, Fairchild Semiconductor was granted the patent on the planar process, the basic technique used by subsequent manufacturers. The patent made both Noyce and Fairchild wealthy.

THE "TRAITOROUS EIGHT" FOUND FAIRCHILD SEMICONDUCTOR

In 1957 Fairchild Camera and Instrument Corporation was considering entering the semiconductor business when eight engineers from the Shockley Semiconductor Laboratory in Palo Alto, Calif., resigned en masse because of the management regime of founder William Shockley, coinventor of the transistor. Led by Robert Noyce and Gordon Moore, the group—which Shockley called the "traitorous eight"—presented themselves to Fairchild. Each engineer agreed to contribute $500 of his own money as a stake in the venture. (When the eight later sold their stakes back to Fairchild, each received $250,000.)

Fairchild Semiconductor's first products were silicon-based transistors for military and later industrial applications. Jean Hoerni, one of the founding engineers, realized that depositing a silicon-oxide film on the silicon wafers from which the transistors were cut would reduce the contamination that had plagued production. Noyce took Hoerni's development one step further. Noyce realized that, rather than cut the silicon wafer into individual transistors, different components could be created in the same wafer and connected along the surface by the deposition of a line of conductive metal (a "wire"). He thus conceived the method for making an integrated circuit. Although Fairchild filed a patent application in 1959 for this planar process, it soon cross-licensed integrated circuit patents with coinventor Texas Instruments while the companies battled in the courts to a split decision 10 years later. Unlike Texas Instruments, Noyce did not use military funding to develop the company's initial manufacturing techniques.

In 1961 Fairchild brought the integrated circuit (IC) to market at a price of $120 per chip. At that time, however, any electronics firm could wire together high-end transistors to produce the same circuits for much less. A buyer had to have a serious space constraint to justify purchasing ICs. Fortunately for Fairchild, the U.S. space program had just such a problem, and the IC was the solution. By 1969 the Apollo program alone had purchased one million silicon chips, a significant fraction of them manufactured by Fairchild.

By the time Noyce and Moore left in 1968 to found Intel Corporation, former Fairchild Semiconductor employees had started dozens of new electronics companies, including National

Semiconductor Corporation, Advanced Micro Devices Inc., and LSI Logic Corporation, in the surrounding region—an area now known as Silicon Valley. Companies descended from Fairchild were often referred to as Fairchildren.

In 1968 Noyce and Moore left Fairchild Semiconductor to start their own company. Soon they were joined by Andrew Grove, another Fairchild colleague, and formed Intel Corporation. In 1971 Intel introduced the first microprocessor, which combined on a single silicon chip the circuitry for both information storage and information processing. Intel quickly became the leading producer of microprocessor chips.

Noyce served as president of Intel until 1975 and then as chairman of the board of directors. In 1978 he stepped down to become chairman of the Semiconductor Industry Association (SIA).

The SIA was formed to address the growing economic concerns of the American semiconductor industry, especially with respect to foreign competition. Noyce played an important role in establishing Sematech, a joint industry-government consortium formed with sometimes conflicting goals—research to keep the American semiconductor industry at the forefront and efforts to maintain a domestic semiconductor manufacturing capacity. Noyce became Sematech Inc.'s first president in 1988.

Noyce held 16 patents and was awarded the National Medal of Science in 1979. A lifelong swimmer (and former Iowa state diving champion), Noyce died of a heart attack following a morning swim in 1990.

CHAPTER 23

GORDON MOORE

Born Jan. 3, 1929, San Francisco, Calif., U.S.

American engineer Gordon Earle Moore was a cofounder, with Robert Noyce, of Intel Corporation in 1968.

Moore studied chemistry at the University of California at Berkeley (B.S., 1950), and in 1954 he received a Ph.D. in chemistry and physics from the California Institute of Technology (Caltech), Pasadena. After graduation, Moore joined the Applied Physics Laboratory at Johns Hopkins University in Laurel, Md., where he examined the physical chemistry of solid rocket propellants used by the U.S. Navy in antiaircraft missiles. Moore soon decided that private industry offered more exciting research with greater potential rewards.

Moore was particularly excited about the potential of the transistor, a recent invention awaiting the development of practical manufacturing techniques. In 1956 Moore returned to California to work at Shockley Semiconductor Laboratory, which William Shockley, one of the Nobel Prize-winning inventors of the transistor, had just opened in Palo Alto. The new laboratory was researching manufacturing methods for silicon-based transistors, but after a hectic year-and-a-half under Shockley's management—capped by an appeal by Moore and others that the company hire a professional manager—Moore and seven colleagues resigned and joined with Fairchild Camera and Instrument Corporation to form a new company, Fairchild Semiconductor Corporation, in Santa Clara. In 1957 Fairchild was looking to enter the transistor business, and the "traitorous eight"—as Shockley named the defectors—presented themselves as a prepackaged solution. With Fairchild's financing and investments from each of the founding members, the new company soon emerged as a major transistor manufacturer. Moore became director of the new company's research and development in 1959, after cofounder Robert Noyce (coinventor of the integrated circuit) was elevated from that post to general manager.

During his years at Fairchild, it became clear to Moore that, no matter how much science went into conceiving of silicon wafers, there would always be an artlike skill associated with their production. When Moore and Noyce left Fairchild in 1968 to establish Intel Corporation (also located in Santa Clara), they decided to merge theory and practice by forcing research scientists and engineers to work directly on the production of chips, especially the magnetic oxide semiconductor memory chips that became Intel's first big commercial success.

Moore was vice president (1968–75), president (1975–79), chief executive officer (1975–87), and chairman of the board of directors (1979–97) of Intel. In 1993 he became chairman of the board of trustees of Caltech. Moore was awarded the National Medal of Technology in 1990.

In spite of the aforementioned accomplishments, Moore may be best known for a rather simple observation. In 1965, for a special issue of the journal *Electronics*, Moore was asked to predict developments over the next decade. In reviewing past increases in the number of transistors per silicon chip, Moore formulated what became known as Moore's law: the number of transistors per silicon chip doubles each year. In 1975, as the rate of growth began to slow, Moore revised his time frame to two years. His revised law was a bit pessimistic; over roughly 40 years from 1961, the number of transistors doubled approximately every 18 months. Magazines regularly referred to Moore's law as though it were inexorable—a technological law with the assurance of Newton's laws of motion. Only time will tell if Moore's law will be repealed.

CHAPTER 24

MANUEL BLUM

Born April 26, 1938, Caracas, Venez.

Venezuelan-born American mathematician and computer scientist Manuel Blum was the winner of the 1995 A.M. Turing Award, computer science's most prestigious honour, in "recognition of his contributions to the foundations of computational complexity theory and its application to cryptography and program checking."

Blum earned a bachelor's degree (1959) and a master's degree (1961) in electrical engineering and a doctorate (1964) in mathematics from the Massachusetts Institute of Technology. After finishing his studies, Blum joined the computer science department at the University of California, Berkeley. In 1999 Carnegie Mellon University succeeded in recruiting Blum and his wife, Lenore, from Berkeley's computer science department. An important motivation for them to leave their professorships at Berkeley was the chance to join their son, Avrim Blum, who had joined Carnegie Mellon's computer science department in 1991. The parents moved into offices on either side of their son, and all three have collaborated on several computer science projects. In particular, the three are part of the ALADDIN (*al*gorithm *ad*aptation *d*issemination and *int*egration) project, which received funding from the U.S. National Science Foundation for matching algorithms developed in academia with potential industrial applications.

CAPTCHA

A CAPTCHA is a visual interface feature, or code, to stop automated computer programs, known as bots and spiders, from gaining access to Web sites. A CAPTCHA, which may consist of letters, numbers, or images, is distorted in some manner to prevent recognition by computers but not so distorted that a human with normal vision cannot identify the code and retype it.

In 2000 Yahoo! Inc., an American Internet services company, was having trouble keeping computer programs that were pretending to be teenagers out of its chat rooms, where the programs were collecting personal information and adding spam. Yahoo! contacted the computer science department at Carnegie Mellon University for help. Manuel Blum, together with Luis von Ahn, Nicholas Hopper, and John Langford, came up with the first CAPTCHA—an acronym for "completely automated public Turing test to tell computers and humans apart."

As computer programs became more sophisticated, the early simple techniques of using overlapping letters and various background colours and patterns were replaced by using ever more broken or partial typefaces and highly distorted script characters. Carried to an extreme, many people found they could no longer read CAPTCHAs, which led to the development of CAPTCHAs based on identifying some object, such as a type of animal, from a photograph. The development of CAPTCHAs has spurred research in visual recognition, a field in artificial intelligence that has applications in optical scanning software, remote sensing, and robotics.

In 2000 Yahoo! Inc., an American Internet search engine company, contacted the computer science department at Carnegie Mellon for help in distinguishing human and computer visitors to its Web site. Manuel Blum was one of the scientists who took up the challenge, which led to the creation of the CAPTCHA (completely automated public Turing test to tell computers and humans apart). As sophisticated computer programs have been developed to

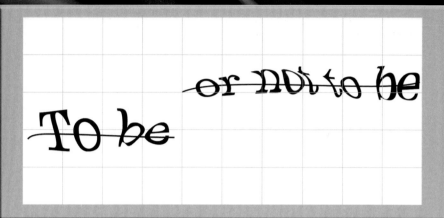

Manuel Blum helped develop the CAPTCHA (completely automated public Turing test to tell computers and humans apart). Shutterstock.com

discern simply disguised words in CAPTCHAs, Blum and others have continued to experiment with more complex distortions that test the limits of human recognition.

Blum was elected to the American Association for the Advancement of Science (1988), the American Academy of Arts and Sciences (1995), the U.S. National Academy of Sciences (2002), and the U.S. National Academy of Engineering (2006).

CHAPTER 25

ROBERT KAHN AND VINTON CERF

Respectively, born Dec. 23, 1938, Brooklyn, N.Y., U.S.; born June 23, 1943, New Haven, Conn., U.S.

In 2004 American electrical engineer Robert Elliot Kahn and American computer scientist Vinton Gray Cerf won the A.M. Turing Award, the highest honour in computer science, for their "pioneering work on internetworking, including the design and implementation of the Internet's basic communications protocols, TCP/IP (Transmission Control Protocol/Internet Protocol), and for inspired leadership in networking." For their work on TCP/IP, Kahn and Cerf are frequently referred to as the "founders of the Internet."

In 1965 Cerf received a bachelor's degree in mathematics from Stanford University in California. He then worked for IBM as a systems engineer before attending the University of California at Los Angeles (UCLA), where he earned a master's degree in computer science in 1970. He returned to Stanford and completed a doctorate in computer science in 1972.

While at UCLA, Cerf wrote the communication protocol for the ARPANET (Advanced Research Projects Agency Network), the first computer network based on packet switching, a heretofore untested technology. UCLA was among the four original ARPANET nodes. While working on the protocol, Cerf met Kahn, an electrical engineer who was then a senior scientist at Bolt Beranek & Newman. Cerf's professional relationship with Kahn was among the most important of his career.

Kahn, after receiving an engineering degree from City College of New York in 1960, received a master's degree (1962) and a doctorate (1964) in electrical engineering from Princeton University. Immediately after completing his doctorate, he worked for Bell Laboratories and subsequently served as an assistant professor of electrical engineering at the Massachusetts Institute of Technology (MIT) from 1964 to 1966. However, it was his role as a senior scientist at Bolt Beranek & Newman (BB&N), an engineering consulting firm located in Cambridge, Mass., that brought Kahn into contact with the planning for a new kind of computer network, the ARPANET.

ARPANET was named for its sponsor, the Defense Advanced Research Projects Agency, or DARPA. The network was based on a radically different architecture known as packet switching, in which messages were split

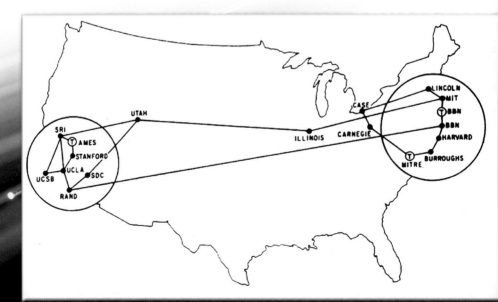

The ARPANET (Advanced Research Projects Agency Network) was based on packet switching technology. This early 1970s map shows communication centres and relays. Apic/Hulton Archive/Getty Images

into multiple "packets" that traveled independently over many different circuits to their common destination. (By contrast, in ordinary telephone communications a specific circuit must be dedicated to the transmission.) ARPANET is frequently referred to as a predecessor of the Internet, but it was more than that—it was the common technological context in which an entire generation of computer scientists came of age. While at BB&N, Kahn had two major accomplishments. First, he was part of a group that designed the network's Interface Message Processor, which would mediate between the network and each institution's host computer. Second, and perhaps more important, in 1972 Kahn helped organize the first International Conference on Computer Communication, which served as the ARPANET's public debut.

In 1972 Kahn left BB&N for DARPA's Information Processing Techniques Office (IPTO). There he confronted a set of problems related to the deployment of packet switching technology in military radio and satellite communications. However, the real technical problem lay in connecting these disparate military networks—hence the name Internet for a "network of networks." In 1973 Kahn approached Cerf, then a professor at Stanford, to assist him in designing this new network. Cerf and Kahn soon worked out a preliminary version of what they called the ARPA Internet, the details of which they published as a joint paper in 1974. Cerf joined Kahn at IPTO in 1976 to manage the office's networking projects. Together they produced TCP/IP, an electronic transmission protocol that separated packet error checking (TCP) from issues related to domains and destinations (IP). The protocol is the basis for the Internet's open architecture, which permits any computer with the appropriate connection to enter the network.

In addition to his work on the Internet, Kahn was the designer of the U.S. military's Strategic Computing Initiative during the administration of Pres. Ronald Reagan. Kahn also coined the phrase "national information infrastructure" during this period. Upon leaving IPTO in 1985, Kahn served as president of the Corporation for National Research Initiatives, a not-for-profit group located in Reston, Va., and dedicated to the development of network technologies for the public.

Cerf's work on making the Internet a publicly accessible medium continued after he left DARPA in 1982 to become a vice president at MCI Communications Corporation. While at MCI he led the effort to develop and deploy MCI Mail, the first commercial e-mail service to use the Internet. In 1986 Cerf became a vice president at the Corporation for National Research Initiatives. Cerf also served as founding president of the Internet Society from 1992 to 1995. In 1994 Cerf returned to MCI as a senior vice president, and from 1998 to 2007 he served as the first chairman of the Internet Corporation for Assigned Names and Numbers (ICANN), the group that oversees the Internet's growth and expansion. In 2005 he left MCI to become vice president and "chief Internet evangelist" at the search engine company Google Inc.

In addition to his work on the Internet, Cerf served on many government panels related to cybersecurity and the national information infrastructure. A fan of science fiction, he was a technical consultant to one of author Gene Roddenberry's posthumous television projects, *Earth: Final Conflict*.

Among the many honours given them for their role in developing the Internet, Kahn and Cerf received the U.S. National Academy of Engineering's Charles Stark Draper Prize (2001) and the Presidential Medal of Freedom (2005).

CHAPTER 26

DENNIS RITCHIE AND KEN THOMPSON

Respectively, born Sept. 9, 1941, Bronxville, Eastchester, N.Y., U.S.; born Feb. 4, 1943, New Orleans, La., U.S.

In 1983 American computer scientists Dennis MacAlistair Ritchie and Kenneth Lane Thompson were awarded computer science's prestigious A.M. Turing Award for "their development of generic operating systems theory and specifically for the implementation of the UNIX operating system." UNIX is widely used for Internet servers, workstations, and mainframe computers.

Ritchie earned a bachelor's degree (1963) in physics and a doctorate (1968) in mathematics from Harvard University. In 1967 he joined Bell Labs, where he first worked on the Multics operating system (OS). Thompson earned a bachelor's degree (1965) and a master's degree (1966) in electrical engineering from the University of California, Berkeley. After graduation, he went to work at Bell Labs, where he too worked on Multics. Multics was a time-sharing system funded by the Advanced Research Projects Agency and jointly developed by researchers at the Massachusetts Institute of Technology, Bell Labs, and General Electric Co. However, AT&T Corporation (then the parent company of Bell Labs) withdrew from the project and removed its GE computers in 1969.

Thompson had written an electronic game, *Space Travel*, for Multics, which he wanted to play on Bell Labs' obsolete Digital Equipment Corporation PDP-7 minicomputer. So upon AT&T's withdrawal from the Multics project, he began developing a more flexible OS for the

PDP-7. Within a few months, Thompson and Ritchie, who had joined him, had created UNIX, a new OS not completely tied to any particular computer hardware, as earlier systems had been.

In conjunction with the development of UNIX, Thompson, with some help from Ritchie, in 1970 created the B programming language. As they moved their system to a newer PDP-11 minicomputer in 1971, the shortcomings of B became apparent, and Ritchie extended the language over the next year to create the C programming language. C and its family of languages, including C++ and Java, remain among the most widely used computer programming languages. In 1973 Thompson and Ritchie rewrote UNIX in C.

Thompson left Bell Laboratories for a while and taught a course on UNIX at the University of California, Berkeley, in the mid-1970s. Students and professors there further enhanced UNIX, eventually creating a version of UNIX called Berkeley Software Distribution (BSD). Work at AT&T also continued, leading to the 1983 release of a new version of UNIX called System V. These versions were later joined by UNIX versions created by Sun Microsystems Inc. and Silicon Graphics Inc. among other companies, and continued development kept UNIX on pace with improvements in computer technology. UNIX served as the inspiration for free open-source operating systems such as Linux and FreeBSD, and it is the basis for Apple Inc.'s Mac OS X. The main features of UNIX—its portability (the ability to run on many different systems), multitasking and multiuser capabilities, and its extensive library of software—make it as relevant and useful today as it was in 1969.

Both Ritchie and Thompson were named Bell Labs fellows in 1983, the year they were given the Turing Award. In 1990 Ritchie was appointed head of the System

Software Research Department at Bell Labs, where he led the development of the Plan 9 (1995) and Inferno (1996) operating systems. Among his publications were the *Unix Programmer's Manual* (1971) and, with Brian W. Kernighan, *The C Programming Language* (1988).

In 1980 Belle, a computer chess program that Thompson had developed with Joseph H. Condon, another engineer at Bell Labs, won the World Computing Chess Championship. Also, Thompson assisted Ritchie in the creation of Plan 9 and Inferno. In 1998 the two were awarded the U.S. National Medal of Technology for their development of UNIX. Thompson retired from Bell Labs in December 2000.

CHAPTER 27

CHARLES THACKER

Born Feb. 26, 1943, Pasadena, Calif., U.S.

American physicist and engineer Charles P. Thacker was the winner of the 2009 A.M. Turing Award, the highest honour in computer science, for his "pioneering design and realization of the first modern personal computer."

Thacker received a bachelor's degree in physics from the University of California, Berkeley, in 1967. He then worked at that university for Project Genie, one of the first time-sharing systems in which multiple people could work on the same computer. He and several of his collaborators on Project Genie joined the newly established Xerox Palo Alto Research Center (Xerox PARC) in Palo Alto, Calif., in 1970.

At Xerox PARC, Thacker led the project that developed the Alto, the first personal computer, in 1973. Alto used a bitmap display in which everything on the computer screen was, in effect, a picture and had a graphical user interface in which programs were shown in windows that could be manipulated by using a mouse. However, the mindset at Xerox, like that of many computer manufacturers of that time, was that a market did not exist for such machines. Corporate analysts asserted that Alto, which cost $12,000 to make, would be too expensive to market to the private and small-business users it was designed to serve. Therefore, the machine was never released. Thacker was also part of the team that invented the computer

Charles Thacker worked with Microsoft Corporation on the development of its Tablet PC. Comstock/Thinkstock

networking technology Ethernet, and he designed SIL, one of the first computer-aided design (CAD) programs.

In 1983 Thacker joined Digital Equipment Corporation's System Research Center in Palo Alto. There he led the team that developed Firefly, the first workstation that had more than one processor. In 1997 he joined Microsoft Corporation and established its first research lab in Cambridge, Eng. At Microsoft, he worked on the Tablet PC and did research into computer architecture.

CHAPTER 28

NARAYANA MURTHY

Born Aug. 20, 1946, Kolar, Karnataka state, India.

Indian software entrepreneur Narayana Murthy cofounded Infosys Technologies Ltd., the first Indian company to be listed on an American stock exchange.

Murthy earned a bachelor's degree in electrical engineering from the University of Mysore in 1967 and a master's degree in technology from the Indian Institute of Technology, Kanpur, in 1969. During the 1970s he worked in Paris, where, among other projects, he helped design an operating system for handling air cargo at Charles de Gaulle Airport. Returning to India, he accepted a position with a computer systems company in Pune, but eventually he decided to launch his own company. He cofounded Infosys with six fellow computer professionals in 1981.

The company grew slowly until the early 1990s, when the Indian government's decisive move toward economic liberalization and deregulation contributed to dramatic growth in the country's high-technology and computer sectors. Murthy aggressively expanded his company's services and client base, negotiating deals with many overseas businesses to provide them with consulting, systems integration, software development, and product engineering services. By 1999 Infosys had joined NASDAQ, becoming the first Indian company to be listed on an American stock exchange. The following year *Asiaweek* included Murthy in its Power 50, the

Narayana Murthy was one of the cofounders of Infosys Technologies Ltd., the first Indian company to be listed on NASDAQ. The India Today Group/ Getty Images

magazine's annual list of the most powerful people in the region. In addition, *BusinessWeek* named him one of its "Stars of Asia" for three consecutive years (1998–2000), and he was *Fortune* magazine's 2003 Asian Businessman of the Year.

In April 2004 Murthy announced that the Bangalore-based Infosys had posted $1.06 billion in total annual revenues—an astonishing 33 percent increase in revenues over the previous fiscal year. The company's growth was all the more remarkable because it came in the midst of a global downturn in the information technology industry. Such phenomenal success was not without controversy, however. A political debate erupted in the United States over job losses caused by offshoring, the outsourcing of work overseas. This was of serious concern to Infosys, which derived more than two-thirds of its revenue from American corporations. Murthy responded that it was "normal" that concerns over job losses would be voiced, and while he indicated that he thought outsourcing was "here to stay," he made efforts to assuage some of the anger by announcing that Infosys would establish a consulting unit in the United States that would employ 500 workers. In the end the controversy appeared not to have significantly dented Infosys's business. When Murthy retired in 2006, he left behind a company with some 70,000 employees and $3 billion a year in revenues. He was awarded the Legion of Honour in 2008.

CHAPTER 29

STEPHEN WOZNIAK

Born Aug. 11, 1950, San Jose, Calif., U.S.

American electronics engineer Stephen Gary Wozniak was a cofounder, with Steven P. Jobs, of Apple Computer. He also designed the first commercially successful personal computer.

Wozniak—or "Woz," as he was commonly known—was the son of an electrical engineer for the Lockheed Missiles and Space Company in Sunnyvale, Calif., in what would become known as Silicon Valley. A precocious but undisciplined student with a gift for mathematics and an interest in electronics, he attended the University of Colorado at Boulder for one year (1968–69) before dropping out. Following his return to California, he attended a local community college and then the University of California, Berkeley. In 1971 Wozniak designed the "Blue Box," a device for phreaking (hacking into the telephone network without paying for long-distance calls) that he and Jobs, a student at his old high school whom he met about this time, began selling to other students. Also during the early 1970s Wozniak worked at several small electronics firms in the San Francisco Bay area before obtaining a position with the Hewlett-Packard Company in 1975, by which time he had formally dropped out of Berkeley.

Wozniak also became involved with the Homebrew Computer Club, a San Francisco Bay area group centred around the Altair 8800 microcomputer do-it-yourself

Stephen Wozniak. Alberto E. Rodriguez/Getty Images

kit, which was based on one of the world's first micro-processors, the Intel Corporation 8080, released in 1975. While working as an engineering intern at Hewlett-Packard, Wozniak designed his own microcomputer in 1976 using the new microprocessor, but the company was not interested in developing his design. Jobs, who was also a Homebrew member, showed so much enthusiasm for Wozniak's design that they decided to work together, forming their own company, Apple Computer. Their initial capital came from selling Jobs's automobile and Wozniak's programmable calculator, and they set up production in the Jobs family garage to build microcomputer circuit boards. Sales of the kit were promising, so they decided to produce a finished product, the Apple II; completed in 1977, it included a built-in keyboard and support for a colour monitor. The Apple II, which combined Wozniak's brilliant engineering with Jobs's aesthetic sense, was the first personal computer to appeal beyond hobbyist circles. When the company went public in 1980, its market value exceeded $1 billion, at the time the fastest rise to that milestone in corporate history, and Wozniak's stock in the company made him an instant multimillionaire.

During these years, Wozniak designed new hardware components, such as the 3.5-inch floppy disk drive for the Apple II, and various components of the Apple operating system and its software applications. This work ended in 1981 when he crashed his small airplane, leaving him temporarily with traumatic amnesia (unable to form new long-term memories), and he was forced to go on a sabbatical. He soon decided to return to Berkeley, under the pseudonym of Rocky Clark, to finish the computer science and electrical engineering courses needed to earn those degrees. Although he dropped out again, he eventually was given credit for his work at Apple, and the school awarded him a bachelor of science degree in electrical engineering in 1987.

Wozniak returned to Apple in 1982, though he resisted efforts to involve him in management. He finally retired as an active employee in 1985, immediately after being awarded, along with Jobs, a National Medal of Technology by U.S. Pres. Ronald W. Reagan. Wozniak spent the ensuing decades engaged in philanthropic causes, especially involving the education of children, and in volunteer work teaching computer enrichment classes to preteens.

Although Wozniak was semiretired after leaving Apple, he kept up with the computing world by funding various business ventures and occasionally serving as an adviser or board member for different companies. In 2009 he became the chief scientist at Fusion-Io, an American company that produces high-capacity, solid-state storage devices. Wozniak was serving on the company's board of directors when he decided to become a full-time employee.

In 2006 Wozniak published his autobiography, *iWoz: Computer Geek to Cult Icon: How I Invented the Personal Computer, Co-Founded Apple, and Had Fun Doing It.*

CHAPTER 30

RICHARD STALLMAN

Born March 16, 1953, New York, N.Y., U.S.

A merican computer programmer Richard Matthew Stallman, a free-software advocate, was the founder of the Free Software Foundation.

Stallman earned a bachelor's degree in physics from Harvard University in 1974. In 1971, as a freshman at Harvard, he had begun working at the Artificial Intelligence Lab at the Massachusetts Institute of Technology (MIT), where he wrote the Emacs text editor in the C computer programming language with James Gosling (who later developed Java). In 1983 Stallman began working in his personal time on his GNU Project, or GNU operating system. GNU was intended to be a free version of AT&T's UNIX—the name *GNU* was created as a recursive acronym of "GNU's not UNIX."

In 1984 Stallman left MIT over concerns about changes to the university's software copyright rules—he was one of the last of the "hackers," i.e., computer programmers who strongly believed in freely modifying and sharing computer code. In 1985 Stallman created the nonprofit Free Software Foundation, which initially focused on supporting his GNU Project. In 1990 he was awarded a MacArthur Fellowship, the so-called "genius award" that gives recipients a substantial financial stipend with no strings attached. The award helped free Stallman to write various utilities for the GNU Project, such as the GNU Emacs editor, GNU compiler, and GNU debugger, which would later be combined with the kernel developed by Linus Torvalds, a Finnish computer science student, to produce the GNU/Linux, or Linux, operating system in 1994. Stallman's *GNU Emacs Manual*, which has gone through numerous revisions, is freely available from the GNU Web site.

With the release of a free operating system, Stallman and the Free Software Foundation focused on promoting free software and the development of the GNU General Public License (GNU GPL), commonly known as a copyleft agreement, which gives authors a way to allow their works to be modified without releasing them to the public domain.

In 1999 Stallman published "The Free Universal Encyclopedia and Learning Resource," a paper calling for the creation of an open-source encyclopaedia. Almost as soon as he set up the GNUpedia Project, another open-source encyclopaedia project, Nupedia, the predecessor of Wikipedia, appeared and adopted the GNU Free Documentation License, so the work on the GNUpedia Project was merged into Nupedia.

True to his hacker roots, Stallman continued to promote free software around the world. However, he had limited success in convincing governments to move completely to free software.

CHAPTER 31

RODNEY BROOKS

Born Dec. 30, 1954, Adelaide, S.Aus., Austl.

Rodney Allen Brooks, a computer scientist and artificial intelligence scientist, was the designer of mobile autonomous robots.

While attending Flinders University in Adelaide, S.Aus., where he received bachelor's (1975) and master's degrees (1978) in pure mathematics, Brooks was given access to the university's mainframe computer for 12 hours each Sunday. This experience with computers was enough to convince Brooks to come to America to study with the artificial intelligence (AI) pioneer John McCarthy at Stanford University in California. Brooks chose a traditional AI problem for his doctoral research (1981), which he subsequently expanded and published as *Model-Based Computer Vision* (1984).

By the time Brooks had finished his doctorate and moved to the Mobile Robotics Laboratory at the Massachusetts Institute of Technology (MIT) in 1984, he had become discouraged with AI research, especially with the field's top-down approach to problem solving. The top-down approach, which dominated the field at that time, presupposes that a computer must first be supplied with an internal representation of the "essential" features of the world in which it operates—an immensely difficult framework problem for all but the very simplest tasks. Brooks turned that approach on its head, arguing that research should focus on a bottom-up approach—that is, on action and behaviour rather than on representation and function. Brooks began by building basic robots that could perform the simplest "insect-like" actions. Although no one claims that insects have sophisticated brains, they can engage in rather elaborate behaviours. Similarly, building on a few simple actions and the premise that learning comes from interacting with the real world, Brooks's robots displayed surprisingly complex behaviour.

In 1991 Brooks cofounded the company iRobot, which produced robots for use in the home, the military, and industry. One of its most successful models was the Roomba, a small autonomous robot introduced in 2002 that could vacuum a floor. Another iRobot product, the Packbot, was used by U.S. soldiers in Afghanistan and Iraq to dispose of explosives.

In 1997 Brooks became director of the MIT Artificial Intelligence Research Laboratory, where he continued to push AI in this fundamentally new direction. His influential and accessible essays were collected in *Cambrian Intelligence: The Early History of the New AI* (1999). What initially had appeared heretical to traditional AI eventually became a new orthodoxy, complete with industrial and military applications. Brooks and his students designed robots to explore Mars as well as for more mundane tasks such as clearing minefields. He went on to the project of "raising" a robot "child" named Cog—a clever allusion to cognition and gears—that would learn from its interactions with humans. Work on Cog ended in 2004, but Cog did learn some rudimentary skills, such as recognizing animate objects.

In 2003 the MIT Artificial Intelligence Research Laboratory merged with the Laboratory of Computer Science to form the Computer Science and Artificial Intelligence Laboratory, with Brooks as director. He left iRobot in 2008 to found another robotics company, Heartland Robotics, to build robots for use in manufacturing. He retired from MIT in 2010.

CHAPTER 32

CARLY FIORINA

Born Sept. 6, 1954, Austin, Texas, U.S.

American business executive Carly Fiorina, as chief executive officer (CEO) of Hewlett-Packard Company from 1999 to 2005, was the first woman to head a company listed on the Dow Jones Industrial Average.

Fiorina was born Cara Carleton Sneed, the daughter of Joseph Sneed, a judge and a law professor, and Madelon Sneed, an artist. Her family moved often, and she attended school in Ghana, the United Kingdom, and the U.S. states of North Carolina and California. After graduating from Stanford University in 1976 with a bachelor's degree in medieval history and philosophy, she attended law school at the University of California, Los Angeles, but dropped out after only one semester. She later studied at the University of Maryland, College Park (M.B.A., 1980), and at the Massachusetts Institute of Technology's Sloan School of Management (M.S., 1989).

At age 25 she started in an entry-level position at AT&T Corporation. Within 10 years she was named the company's first female officer, and at age 40 she became head of AT&T's North American operations. (She also later married Frank Fiorina, an AT&T executive.) She engineered the successful spin-off of AT&T's research division as Lucent Technologies Inc. in 1996. Two years later she was promoted to president of Lucent's Global Service Provider Business, in charge of sales to the world's largest telecommunications companies.

Carly Fiorina, 2010. Carly for California

In 1999 Hewlett-Packard Company (HP) announced that Fiorina would become its new CEO—the first outsider to lead HP in its 60-year history. Fiorina encountered some resistance from employees as she updated the "HP Way" of working—a traditional, consensus-based system that she felt had become slow and bureaucratic. Her plan to merge HP, then the second largest computer company in the United States, with Compaq Computer Corporation, then the third largest, was contested by Walter Hewlett and David Packard, the sons of HP's cofounders. Fiorina prevailed, however, winning the support of shareholders by a slim margin of 51.4 percent of the votes cast. In 2002 the two firms merged, retaining the Hewlett-Packard name. The deal, however, failed to generate the expected profits, and in 2005 Fiorina was forced to resign as CEO.

After leaving HP, Fiorina published an autobiography, *Tough Choices*, in 2006. She also served as a commentator for Fox News and as a consultant to the 2008 U.S. presidential campaign of Sen. John McCain. In November 2009 Fiorina announced that she was running for the U.S. Senate, and she secured the nomination with a commanding victory in the Republican primary in June 2010. In the general election, however, she was defeated by Barbara Boxer.

CHAPTER 33

STEVE JOBS

Born Feb. 24, 1955, San Francisco, Calif., U.S.

Steven Paul Jobs, cofounder of Apple Computer Inc. (now Apple Inc.), is a charismatic pioneer of the personal computer era.

Jobs was raised by adoptive parents in Cupertino, Calif., located in what is now known as Silicon Valley. Though he was interested in engineering, his passions of youth varied. He dropped out of Reed College, in Portland, Ore., took a job at Atari Corporation as a video game designer in early 1974, and saved enough money for a pilgrimage to India to experience Buddhism.

Back in Silicon Valley in the autumn of 1974, Jobs reconnected with Stephen Wozniak, a former high school friend who was working for the Hewlett-Packard Company. When Wozniak told Jobs of his progress in designing his own computer logic board, Jobs suggested that they go into business together, which they did after Hewlett-Packard formally turned down Wozniak's design in 1976. The Apple I, as they called the logic board, was built in the Jobses' family garage with money they obtained by selling Jobs's Volkswagen minibus and Wozniak's programmable calculator.

Jobs was one of the first entrepreneurs to understand that the personal computer would appeal to a broad audience, at least if it did not appear to belong in a junior high school science fair. With Jobs's encouragement, Wozniak designed an improved model, the Apple II, complete with a keyboard, and they arranged to have a sleek, molded plastic case manufactured to enclose the unit.

Steve Jobs ushered Apple into the telecommunications age with the introduction of the iPhone. Jim Watson/AFP/Getty Images

Though Jobs had long, unkempt hair and eschewed business garb, he managed to obtain financing, distribution, and publicity for the company, Apple Computer, incorporated in 1977—the same year that the Apple II was completed. The machine was an immediate success, becoming synonymous with the boom in personal computers. In 1981 the company had a record-setting public stock offering and, in 1983, made the quickest entrance (to that time) into the *Fortune* 500 list of America's top companies. In 1983 the company recruited PepsiCo Inc. president John Sculley to be its chief executive officer (CEO) and, implicitly, Jobs's mentor in the fine points of running a large corporation. Jobs had convinced Sculley to accept the position by challenging him: "Do you want to sell sugar water for the rest of your life?" The line was shrewdly effective, but it also revealed Jobs's own near-messianic belief in the computer revolution.

During that same period, Jobs was heading the most important project in the company's history. In 1979 he led a small group of Apple engineers to a technology demonstration at the Xerox Corporation's Palo Alto Research Center (PARC) to see how the graphical user interface could make computers easier to use and more efficient. Soon afterward, Jobs left the engineering team that was designing Lisa, a business computer, to head a smaller group building a lower-cost computer. Both computers were redesigned to exploit and refine the PARC ideas, but Jobs was explicit in favouring the Macintosh, or Mac, as the new computer became known. Jobs coddled his engineers and referred to them as artists, but his style was uncompromising; at one point he demanded a redesign of an internal circuit board simply because he considered it unattractive. He would later be renowned for his insistence that the Macintosh be not merely great but "insanely great." In January 1984 Jobs himself introduced the Macintosh in a brilliantly choreographed demonstration that was the centrepiece of an extraordinary publicity campaign. It would later be pointed to as the archetype of "event marketing."

However, the first Macs were underpowered and expensive, and they had few software applications—all of which resulted in disappointing sales. Apple steadily improved the machine, so that it eventually became the company's lifeblood as well as the model for all subsequent computer interfaces. But Jobs's apparent failure to correct the problem quickly led to tensions in the company, and in 1985 Sculley convinced Apple's board of directors to remove the company's famous cofounder.

Jobs quickly started another firm, the NeXT Corporation, designing powerful workstation computers for the education market. His funding partners included Texan entrepreneur Ross Perot and Canon Inc., a Japanese electronics company. Although the Next computer was notable for its engineering design, it was eclipsed by less costly computers from competitors such as Sun Microsystems Inc. In the early 1990s, Jobs focused the company on its innovative software system, NextStep.

Meanwhile, in 1986 Jobs bought Pixar Animation Studios, a computer-graphics firm founded by Hollywood movie director George Lucas. Over the following decade Jobs built Pixar into a major animation studio that, among other achievements, produced the first full-length feature film to be completely computer-animated, *Toy Story*, in 1995. Also in 1995, Pixar's public stock offering made Jobs, for the first time, a billionaire.

In late 1996, Apple, saddled by huge financial losses and on the verge of collapse, hired a new chief executive, semiconductor executive Gilbert Amelio. When Amelio learned that the company, following intense and prolonged research efforts, had failed to develop an acceptable replacement for the Macintosh's aging operating system (OS), he chose NextStep, buying Jobs's company for more than $400 million—and bringing Jobs back to Apple as a consultant. However, Apple's board of directors soon became disenchanted with Amelio's inability to turn the company's finances around and in June 1997 requested Apple's prodigal cofounder to lead the company once again. Jobs quickly forged an alliance with Apple's erstwhile foe, the Microsoft Corporation, scrapped Amelio's Mac-clone agreements, and simplified the company's product line. He also engineered an award-winning advertising campaign that urged potential customers to "think different" and buy Macintoshes. Just as important is what he did not do: he resisted the temptation to make machines that ran Microsoft's Windows OS; nor did he, as some urged, spin off Apple as a software-only company. Jobs believed that Apple, as the only major personal computer maker with its own operating system, was in a unique position to innovate.

Innovate he did. In 1998, Jobs introduced the iMac, an egg-shaped, one-piece computer that offered high-speed processing at a relatively modest price and initiated a trend of high-fashion computers. (Subsequent models sported five different bright colours.) By the end of the year, the iMac was the nation's highest-selling personal computer, and Jobs was able to announce consistent profits for the once-moribund company. The following year, he triumphed once more with the stylish iBook, a laptop computer built with students in mind, and the G4, a desktop computer sufficiently powerful that (so Apple boasted) it could not be exported under certain circumstances because it qualified as a supercomputer. Though Apple did not regain the industry dominance it once had, Steve Jobs had saved his company, and in the process reestablished himself as a master high-technology marketer and visionary.

THE GUI

There was no one inventor of the graphical user interface, or GUI, a computer program that enables a person to communicate with a computer through the use of symbols, visual metaphors, and pointing devices. Instead, the GUI evolved with the help of a series of innovators, each improving on a predecessor's work. The first theorist was Vannevar Bush, director of the U.S. Office of Scientific Research and Development, who in an influential essay, "As We May Think," published in the July 1945 issue of the *Atlantic Monthly*, envisioned how future information gatherers would use a computerlike device, which he called a "memex," outfitted with buttons and levers that could access vast amounts of linked data—an idea that anticipated hyperlinking.

Bush's essay enchanted Douglas Engelbart, a young naval technician, who embarked on a lifelong quest to realize some of those ideas. While at the Stanford Research Institute (now known as SRI International), working on a U.S. Department of Defense grant, Engelbart formed the Augmentation Research Center. By the mid-1960s it had devised a set of innovations, including a way of segmenting the monitor screen so that it appeared to be a viewpoint into a document. (The use of multiple tiles, or windows, on the screen could easily accommodate different documents, something that Bush thought crucial.) Engelbart's team also invented a pointing device known as a "mouse," then a palm-sized wooden block on wheels whose movement controlled a cursor on the computer screen. These innovations allowed information to be manipulated in a more flexible, natural manner than the prevalent method of typing one of a limited set of commands.

The next wave of GUI innovation occurred at the Xerox Corporation's Palo Alto (California) Research Center (PARC), to which several of Engelbart's team moved in the 1970s. The new interface ideas found their way to a computer workstation called the Xerox Star, which was introduced in 1981. Though the process was expensive, the Star (and its prototype predecessor, the Alto) used a technique called "bit mapping" in which everything on the computer screen was, in effect, a picture. Bit mapping not only welcomed the use of graphics but allowed the computer screen to display exactly what would be output from a printer—a feature that became known as "what you see is what you get," or WYSIWYG.

The computer scientists at PARC, notably Alan Kay, also designed the Star interface to embody a metaphor: a set of small pictures, or "icons," were arranged on the screen, which was to be thought of as a virtual desktop. The icons represented officelike activities such as retrieving files from folders and printing documents. By using the mouse to position the computer's cursor over an icon and then clicking a button on the mouse, a command would be instantly implemented—an intuitively simpler, and generally quicker, process than typing commands.

In late 1979 a group of engineers from Apple, led by cofounder Steven P. Jobs, saw the GUI during a visit to PARC and were sufficiently impressed to integrate the ideas into two new computers, Lisa and Macintosh, then in the design stage. Each product came to have a bit-mapped screen and a sleek, palm-sized mouse (though for simplicity this used a single command button in contrast to the multiple buttons on the SRI and PARC versions). The software interface used overlapping windows, rather than tiling the screen, and featured icons that fit the Xerox desktop metaphor. Moreover, the Apple engineers added their own innovations, including a "menu bar" that, with the click of a mouse, would lower a "pull-down" list of commands. Other touches included scroll bars on the sides of windows and animation when windows opened and closed. Apple even employed a visual artist to create an attractive on-screen "look and feel."

Whereas the Lisa first brought the principles of the GUI into a wider marketplace, it was the lower-cost Macintosh, shipped in 1984, that won millions of converts to the interface. Nonetheless, some critics charged that, because of the higher costs and slower speeds, the GUI was more appropriate for children than for professionals and that the latter would continue to use the old command-line interface of Microsoft's DOS (disk operating system). It was only after 1990, when Microsoft released Windows 3.0 OS, with the first acceptable GUI for International Business Machines Corporation (IBM) PC-compatible computers, that the GUI became the standard interface for personal computers.

In 2001 Jobs started reinventing Apple for the 21st century. That was the year that Apple introduced iTunes, a computer program for playing music and for converting music to the compact MP3 digital format commonly used in computers and other digital devices. Later the same year, Apple began selling the iPod, a portable MP3 player, which quickly became the market leader. In 2003

Apple began selling downloadable copies of major record company songs in MP3 format over the Internet. By 2006 more than one billion songs and videos had been sold through Apple's online iTunes Store. In recognition of the growing shift in the company's business, Jobs officially changed the name of the company to Apple Inc. on Jan. 9, 2007.

In 2007 Jobs took the company into the telecommunications business with the introduction of the touch-screen iPhone, a mobile telephone with capabilities for playing MP3s and videos and for accessing the Internet. Later that year, Apple introduced the iPod Touch, a portable MP3 and gaming device that included built-in Wi-Fi and an iPhone-like touch screen. Bolstered by the use of the iTunes Store to sell Apple and third-party software, the iPhone and iPod Touch soon boasted more games than any other portable gaming system. Jobs announced in 2008 that future releases of the iPhone and iPod Touch would offer improved game functionality. In an ironic development, Apple, which had not supported game developers in its early years out of fear of its computers not being taken seriously as business machines, was now staking a claim to a greater role in the gaming business to go along with its move into telecommunications.

In 2003 Jobs was diagnosed with a rare form of pancreatic cancer. He put off surgery for about nine months while he tried alternative medicine approaches. In 2004 he underwent major reconstructive surgery, known as the Whipple operation. During the procedure, part of the pancreas, a portion of the bile duct, the gallbladder, and the duodenum are removed, after which what is left of the pancreas, the bile duct, and the intestine is reconnected to direct the gastrointestinal secretions back into the stomach. Following a short recovery, Jobs returned to running Apple.

Throughout 2008 Jobs lost significant weight, which produced considerable speculation that his cancer was back. (The average survival rate for patients who have undergone Whipple operations is only 20 percent at five years.) Perhaps more than those of any other large corporation, Apple's stock market shares are tied to the health of its CEO, which led to demands by investors for full disclosure of his health—especially as the first reasons given for his weight loss seemed insufficient to explain his sickly appearance. On Jan. 9, 2009, Jobs released a statement that he was suffering from a hormonal imbalance for which he was being treated and that he would continue his corporate duties. Less than a week later, however, he announced that he was taking an immediate leave of absence through the end of June to recover his health. Having removed himself, at least temporarily, from the corporate structure, Jobs resumed his previous stance that his health was a private matter and refused to disclose any more details.

In June 2009 the *Wall Street Journal* reported that Jobs had received a liver transplant the previous April. Not disclosed was whether the pancreatic cancer he had been treated for previously had spread to his liver. The operation was performed in Tennessee, where the average waiting period for a liver transplant is 48 days, as opposed to the national average of 306 days. Jobs came back to work on June 29, 2009, fulfilling his pledge to return before the end of June. In January 2011, however, Jobs took another medical leave of absence. In August of that year he resigned as CEO but became chairman. Tim Cook, who had been Apple's chief operating officer, was named CEO of the company.

CHAPTER 34

TIM BERNERS-LEE

Born June 8, 1955, London, Eng.

Tim Berners-Lee was a British computer scientist, generally credited as the inventor of the World Wide Web. In 2004 he was awarded a knighthood by Queen Elizabeth II of the United Kingdom and the inaugural Millennium Technology Prize (€1 million) by the Finnish Technology Award Foundation.

Computing came naturally to Berners-Lee, as both of his parents worked on the Ferranti Mark I, the first commercial computer. After graduating in 1976 from the University of Oxford, Berners-Lee designed computer software for two years at Plessey Telecommunications Ltd., located in Poole, Dorset, Eng. Following this, he had several positions in the computer industry, including a stint from June to December 1980 as a software engineering consultant at CERN, the European particle physics laboratory in Geneva.

While at CERN, Berners-Lee developed a program for himself, called Enquire, that could store information in files that contained connections ("links") both within and among separate files—a technique that became known as hypertext. After leaving CERN, Berners-Lee worked for Image Computer Systems Ltd., located in Ferndown, Dorset, where he designed a variety of computer systems. In 1984 he returned to CERN to work on the design of the laboratory's computer network, developing procedures that allowed diverse computers to communicate with one another and researchers to control remote machines. In 1989 Berners-Lee drew up a proposal for creating a global hypertext document system that would make use of the Internet. His goal was to provide researchers with the ability to share their results, techniques, and practices without having to exchange e-mail constantly. Instead, researchers would place such information "online," where their peers could immediately retrieve it anytime, day or night. Berners-Lee wrote the software for the first Web server (the central repository for the files to be shared) and the first Web client, or "browser" (the program to access and display files retrieved from the server), between October 1990 and the summer of 1991. The first "killer application" of the Web at CERN was the laboratory's telephone directory—a mundane beginning for one of the technological wonders of the computer age.

From 1991 to 1993 Berners-Lee evangelized the Web. In 1994 in the United States he established the World Wide Web (W3) Consortium at the Massachusetts Institute of Technology's Laboratory for Computer Science. The consortium, in consultation with others, lends oversight to the Web and the development of standards. In 1999 Berners-Lee became the first holder of the 3Com Founders chair at the Laboratory for Computer Science. His numerous other honours include the National Academy of Engineering's prestigious Charles Stark Draper Prize (2007). Berners-Lee is the author, along with Mark Fischetti, of *Weaving the Web: The Original Design and Ultimate Destiny of the World Wide Web* (2000).

CHAPTER 35

BILL GATES

Born Oct. 28, 1955, Seattle, Wash., U.S.

American computer programmer and entrepreneur William Henry Gates III cofounded Microsoft Corporation, the world's largest personal-computer software company.

Gates wrote his first software program at the age of 13. In high school he helped form a group of programmers who computerized their school's payroll system and founded Traf-O-Data, a company that sold traffic-counting systems to local governments. In 1975 Gates, then a sophomore at Harvard University, joined his hometown friend Paul G. Allen to develop software for the first microcomputers. They began by adapting BASIC, a popular programming language used on large computers, for use on microcomputers. With the success of this project, Gates left Harvard during his junior year and, with Allen, formed Microsoft. Gates's sway over the infant microcomputer industry greatly increased when Microsoft licensed an operating system called MS-DOS to International Business Machines Corporation—then the world's biggest computer supplier and industry pacesetter—for use on its first microcomputer, the IBM PC (personal computer). After the machine's release in 1981, IBM quickly set the technical standard for the PC industry, and MS-DOS likewise pushed out competing operating systems. While Microsoft's independence strained relations with IBM, Gates deftly manipulated the larger company so that it became permanently dependent on him for crucial software. Makers of IBM-compatible PCs, or clones, also turned to Microsoft for their basic software. By the start of the 1990s he had become the PC industry's ultimate kingmaker.

Largely on the strength of Microsoft's success, Gates amassed a huge paper fortune as the company's largest individual shareholder. He became a paper billionaire in 1986, and within a decade his net worth had reached into the tens of billions of dollars—making him by some estimates the world's richest private individual. With few interests beyond software and the potential of information technology, Gates at first preferred to stay out of the public eye, handling civic and philanthropic affairs indirectly through one of his foundations. Nevertheless, as Microsoft's power and reputation grew, and especially as it attracted the attention of the U.S. Justice Department's antitrust division, Gates, with some reluctance, became a more public figure. Rivals (particularly in competing companies in Silicon Valley) portrayed him as driven, duplicitous, and determined to profit from virtually every electronic transaction in the world. His supporters, on the other hand, celebrated his uncanny business acumen, his flexibility, and his boundless appetite for finding new ways to make computers and electronics more useful through software.

All these qualities were evident in Gates's nimble response to the sudden public interest in the Internet. Beginning in 1995 and 1996, Gates feverishly refocused Microsoft on the development of consumer and enterprise software solutions for the Internet, developed the Windows CE operating system platform for networking noncomputer devices such as home televisions and personal digital assistants, created the Microsoft Network to compete with America Online and other Internet providers, and, through Gates's company Corbis, acquired the

Bill Gates. Scott Gries/Getty Images

huge Bettmann photo archives and other collections for use in electronic distribution.

In addition to his work at Microsoft, Gates was also known for his charitable work. With his wife, Melinda, he launched the William H. Gates Foundation (renamed the Bill & Melinda Gates Foundation in 1999) in 1994 to fund global health programs as well as projects in the Pacific Northwest. During the latter part of the 1990s, the couple also funded North American libraries through the Gates Library Foundation (renamed Gates Learning Foundation in 1999) and raised money for minority study grants through the Gates Millennium Scholars program. In June 2006 American businessman and philanthropist Warren Buffett announced an ongoing gift to the foundation, which would allow its assets to total roughly $60 billion in the next 20 years. At the beginning of the 21st century, the foundation continued to focus on global health and global development, as well as community and education causes in the United States. After a short transition period, Gates relinquished day-to-day oversight of Microsoft in June 2008 — although he remained chairman of the board — so he could devote more time to the Bill & Melinda Gates Foundation.

It remains to be seen whether Gates's extraordinary success will guarantee him a lasting place in the pantheon of great Americans. At the very least, historians seem likely to view him as a business figure as important to computers as John D. Rockefeller was to oil. Gates himself displayed an acute awareness of the perils of prosperity in his 1995 best seller, *The Road Ahead*, where he observed, "Success is a lousy teacher. It seduces smart people into thinking they can't lose."

CHAPTER 36

DANNY HILLIS

Born Sept. 25, 1956, Baltimore, Md., U.S.

W illiam Daniel Hillis, Jr., an American pioneer of parallel processing computers, was the founder of Thinking Machines Corporation.

The son of a U.S. Air Force epidemiologist, Hillis spent his early years traveling abroad with his family and being homeschooled. Like his father he developed an interest in biology, while his mother nurtured his interest in mathematics. An inveterate tinkerer who invented with whatever was at hand, Hillis, at the age of 9, built his first "computer" out of a phonograph player; he later built a tick-tack-toe-playing computer out of Tinkertoys. The Hillis family returned to Baltimore in 1968 so that Daniel might attend school while his mother started graduate work in biostatistics.

In 1974 Hillis enrolled at the Massachusetts Institute of Technology (MIT) to study neurophysiology. Soon he found his way to the MIT Artificial Intelligence Laboratory, where he met the pioneering artificial intelligence theorist Marvin Minsky. At Minsky's laboratory Hillis and coworkers developed a graphical user interface for the Logo computer programming language for children. While working on Logo, Hillis learned that Minsky was building a computer, so he read the design plans and studied the machine. Minsky was so impressed by Hillis's suggested improvements that he took Hillis on as a student and provided him with a room in his home. Meanwhile, Hillis changed his major to mathematics (B.S., 1978) and then computer science (M.S., 1981).

While working at Minsky's laboratory, Hillis pioneered a new approach to computing. He had long been intrigued by the nature of thought and wanted to make a computer that might help understand human cognition. He found ordinary computers, which executed operations in a sequential fashion on a single processor, to be unwieldy instruments for studying the brain. Hillis imagined that human thought arises from the operations of millions of neurons interacting and working on problems in diverse ways—in computer parlance, massively parallel processing. Although Seymour Cray had built the Cray X-MP (for *multi*processor) in 1982 by linking together two Cray-1 supercomputers, the common wisdom was that a massively parallel computer system would be inherently inefficient. Hillis set about to challenge that idea by building a machine composed of thousands of simple processors programmed to work and interact together. Initially, Hillis wanted to see whether intelligence might arise from such a new architecture, but the concept soon became a business as well as a research topic.

In 1983, with Minsky's encouragement, Hillis founded Thinking Machines Corporation in Cambridge, Mass. Its first product was the Connection Machine, and its first customer the U.S. Department of Defense's Advanced Research Projects Agency (DARPA). The Connection Machine used commercially available processors connected together to perform operations in parallel. In 1985 the first 65,536-processor Connection Machine was completed. It was comparable in computational power to the world's fastest supercomputer, the Cray-2, but vastly cheaper to build. (The Cray machines relied on very expensive custom-designed processors, whereas the Connection Machine used simple one-bit, or off-on, processors.) In 1985 Hillis published his doctoral dissertation as *The Connection Machine*, and in 1988 he earned his Ph.D. In addition, he was the editor of *A New Era in Computation* (1992), and he wrote *The Pattern on the Stone: The Simple Ideas That Make Computers Work* (1998), among other books.

Hillis left Thinking Machines in 1995 to return to MIT as an adjunct professor and to start his own consulting company. (Soon thereafter Thinking Machines Corporation reorganized as a computer software company and stopped building computers.) In 1996 Hillis became the vice president of research and development at the Walt Disney Company's Imagineering Department, where he was already a consultant on the department's primary responsibility of researching and developing, or "imagineering," rides and attractions for Disney's theme parks. Hillis's new position marked the growing convergence of entertainment and computing technology.

In the same year, Hillis and others established the Long Now Foundation, created to develop a multigenerational perspective on many issues facing civilization. The foundation's most famous project was a mechanical clock designed to last for at least 10,000 years—an appropriate challenge for an unconventional and provocative thinker.

CHAPTER 37

MEG WHITMAN

Born Aug. 4, 1956, Spring Harbor, N.Y., U.S.

American business executive Margaret Whitman served from 1998 to 2008 as president and chief executive officer (CEO) of eBay, an online auction company.

Whitman was born and raised on Long Island, New York. She earned an undergraduate degree in economics from Princeton University in 1977 and a master's degree in business administration from Harvard University in 1979. From 1979 to 1981 she worked in brand management for Procter & Gamble in Cincinnati, Ohio. After moving with her husband to California in 1981, she joined the consulting firm Bain & Co. as a vice president and remained there until 1989.

From 1989 to 1992 Whitman served as senior vice president of marketing at the consumer products division of the Walt Disney Co., where she played a major role in Disney's acquisition of *Discover* magazine. In 1992 she moved to Boston, where she became president of the children's shoe manufacturer Stride Rite. Leaving Stride Rite in 1995, she accepted an offer to become CEO of Florists Transworld Delivery (FTD), a federation of commercial florists. There Whitman encountered opposition from staff members and member florists, who strongly objected to FTD's transformation into a privately held firm. She resigned from FTD in 1997 and became general manager of the Playskool division of the toy and game manufacturer Hasbro.

Meg Whitman, chief executive officer (CEO) of the online auction company eBay, transformed the 12-employee company into a major corporation. Frederick M. Brown/Getty Images

In 1998, when a corporate headhunter first approached her to lead the online auction company eBay, Whitman was not interested. A visit to eBay's headquarters and the testimonies of many enthusiastic users impressed her, however, and she accepted the offer to become the company's president and CEO. One of Whitman's first responsibilities in her new position was to prepare the company for its initial public offering (IPO) in September 1998. She brightened the design of eBay's Web pages and walled off all firearm and pornography auctions into separate age-restricted sites. Eventually, eBay banned auctions of firearms and prohibited sales of tobacco, drugs, alcohol, animals, and body parts.

Whitman was described as "relentlessly optimistic," and those who worked with her said that her ability to stay focused and positive set her apart from most executives.

Over the next few years, eBay continued to flourish under her leadership. When many Internet ventures had either failed or were struggling to survive, she managed to elevate the status of eBay from a small business employing a few dozen people to a major corporation employing some 15,000 and bringing in billions of dollars in revenue. Whitman retired from eBay in 2008.

Whitman, a Republican, served as a national cochair of Sen. John McCain's presidential campaign in 2008. The following year she announced that she was running for governor of California. After spending a record-breaking $81 million on her primary campaign, she secured the Republican gubernatorial nomination in June 2010. In the November general election, however, she was defeated by Jerry Brown.

Whitman wrote (with Joan O'C. Hamilton) *The Power of Many: Values for Success in Business and in Life* (2010).

CHAPTER 38

MICHAEL DELL

Born Feb. 23, 1965, Houston, Texas, U.S.

Michael Dell, an American entrepreneur, businessman, and author, is known as the founder and chief executive officer (CEO) of Dell Inc., one of the world's leading sellers of personal computers (PCs).

As a student at the University of Texas at Austin, Dell started his computer business (originally called PCs Limited) in 1984 with $1,000 in start-up capital. By the second half of his freshman year, Dell had sold $80,000 worth of computers. He dropped out of college at age 19 to run his company full-time, eventually going public in 1988. PCs Limited later became the Dell Computer Corporation and ultimately Dell Inc. when the product line expanded to include more than personal computers.

Dell's business philosophy was to gain PC market share through a combination of cutting costs, reducing delivery time, and providing excellent customer service. To do so, he hired experienced executives, both to fill jobs in the company and to act as personal mentors, and he emphasized direct sales outside the usual retail outlets. In 1992 Dell became the youngest CEO in history to have his firm enter *Fortune* magazine's list of the top 500 corporations. In his book *Direct from Dell: Strategies That Revolutionized an Industry* (1999), Dell outlined the story of the company's development and provided strategies applicable to all businesses.

In 2004 Dell stepped down as CEO of the company, but he remained chairman of the board. He served on the

The Dell PC became one of the world's best-selling computers. Junko Kimura/ Getty Images

Foundation Board of the World Economic Forum and the executive committee of the International Business Council. He also was on the U.S. President's Council of Advisors on Science and Technology and sat on the governing board of the Indian School of Business in Hyderabad.

After experiencing setbacks in 2006—including a 4.1-million-unit recall and an overhaul of the customer service division struggling with complaints—Dell Inc. lost the title of world's largest PC manufacturer to Hewlett-Packard. In response, Dell was reinstated as

CEO in 2007 to oversee Dell 2.0, a far-reaching revamp designed to meet the needs of consumers and regain the company's control of the market.

In 1999 Dell and his wife, Susan, formed the Michael & Susan Dell Foundation to manage the investments and philanthropic efforts of the Dell family. Through the foundation, Dell used some of his personal wealth to help children around the world by focusing on health, education, safety, youth development, and early childhood care. The foundation, which by 2005 had an endowment of more than $1 billion, gave millions of dollars to help victims of the 2004 tsunami in southern Asia. In 2006 it donated $50 million to the University of Texas at Austin.

CHAPTER 39

JIMMY WALES

Born Aug. 7, 1966, Huntsville, Ala., U.S.

Jimmy Donal Wales is an American entrepreneur who cofounded *Wikipedia*, a free Internet-based encyclopaedia operating under an open-source management style.

Wales received degrees in finance from Auburn University (B.S.) and the University of Alabama (M.S.). From 1994 to 2000 he was an options trader in Chicago, amassing enough money to allow him to quit and start his own Internet company. Wales was a devotee of objectivism, and in 1989 he began moderating the online *Ayn Rand Philosophy Discussion List*. In March 2000, perhaps inspired by objectivist "openness," he founded a free online encyclopaedia called *Nupedia*, which sought free contributions from scholars and other experts and subjected them to an intensive peer-review process. Frustrated by the slow progress of this project, Wales and *Nupedia*'s editor in chief, Larry Sanger, in 2001 turned to a new technology, a type of software called wiki, to create *Wikipedia*, a companion encyclopaedia site that anyone could contribute to and edit. Sanger and Wales parted company in 2002, but they continued to dispute who first came up with the idea of using the wiki software.

Despite certain vulnerabilities—including the fact that *Wikipedia* was the object of deliberate vandalism, editorial wars, and practical jokes—the site was a huge success. By 2006 *Wikipedia* was available in a number of languages and was one of the Internet's most popular sites.

WIKIWIKI!

A wiki is a World Wide Web (WWW) site that can be modified or contributed to by users. Wikis can be dated to 1995, when American computer programmer Ward Cunningham created a new collaborative technology for organizing information on Web sites. Using a Hawaiian term meaning "quick," he called this new software WikiWikiWeb, attracted by its alliteration and also by its matching abbreviation (WWW).

Wikis were inspired in part by Apple's HyperCard program, which allowed users to create virtual "card stacks" of information with a host of connections, or links, among the various cards. HyperCard in turn drew upon an idea suggested by Vannevar Bush in his 1945 *Atlantic Monthly* article "As We May Think." There Bush envisioned the memex, a machine that would allow readers to annotate and create links between articles and books recorded on microfilm. HyperCard's "stacks" implemented a version of Bush's vision, but the program relied upon the user to create both the text and the links. For example, one might take a musical score of a symphony and annotate different sections with different cards linked together.

Bush also had imagined that memex users might share what he called "trails," a record of their individual travels through a textual universe. Cunningham's wiki software expanded this idea by allowing users to comment on and change one another's text. Perhaps the best-known use of wiki software is Wikipedia, an online encyclopaedia using the model of open-source software development. Individuals write articles and post them on Wikipedia, and these articles are then open for vetting and editing by the community of Wikipedia readers, rather than by a single editor and fact-checker. Just as open-source software—such as the Linux operating system and the Firefox Web browser—has been developed by nonprofit communities, so too is Wikipedia a nonprofit effort.

For those who challenge this model of development, Cunningham and his followers have adopted an interesting position. It is always going to be the case that certain individuals will maliciously attempt to thwart open-source Web sites such as Wikipedia by introducing false or misleading content. Rather than worrying about every user's actions and intentions, proponents of wiki software rely on their community of users to edit and correct what are perceived to be errors or biases. Although such a system is certainly far from foolproof, wikis stand as an example of the origin of an Internet counterculture that has a basic assumption of the goodness of people.

In addition to encyclopaedias, wiki software is used in a wide variety of contexts to facilitate interaction and cooperation in projects at various scales. Manuals have been written using the wiki model, and individuals have adapted wiki software to serve as personal information organizers on personal computers. It remains to be seen to what extent wiki software will provide a foundation for what some computer scientists refer to as Web 2.0, the web of social software that will enmesh users in both their real and virtual-reality workplaces.

In 2003 Wales established the Wikimedia Foundation to oversee his expanding online enterprises. He extended the wiki model to several other projects, including *Wiktionary* and *Wikinews*. In 2004 he cofounded with Angela Beesley the for-profit Wikia, Inc.

CHAPTER 40

NIKLAS ZENNSTRÖM AND JANUS FRIIS

Respectively, born Feb. 16, 1966, Sweden; born June 26, 1976, Denmark.

Niklas Zennström and Janus Friis, two Scandinavian e-commerce entrepreneurs, created various Internet businesses, notably KaZaA, Skype, and Joost.

Zennström earned a bachelor's degree in business administration and a master's degree in engineering physics and computer science from Uppsala University in Sweden. In 1991 he began working at Tele2, a Swedish telecommunications firm, and in 1997 he hired Friis to head customer service at the Danish branch of Tele2 that Zennström managed at that time. Friis was a high school dropout who taught himself computer skills while employed on the customer help desk at Cybercity, an early Internet service provider (ISP) in Denmark. Soon after he was hired by Zennström, the pair began collaborating on their own business ventures, starting with the ISP Get2Net and a Web portal, Everyday.com.

In 2000 Zennström and Friis created KaZaA, a second-generation peer-to-peer (P2P) file-sharing application that they distributed for free, though it was notoriously loaded with adware (typically, software that generates pop-up ads), spyware (programs that monitor users' actions), and other malware applications that were secretly installed on users' computers. Exactly how much revenue this generated for the company is unknown. KaZaA sought to achieve the popularity of Napster, a first-generation P2P file-sharing application that in 2001 was ordered to shut down following legal challenges in the United States from music and film companies concerned with the software being used for computer piracy. Although Zennström and Friis had hoped to avoid the problems encountered by Napster, their company was sued almost immediately in Dutch courts for copyright infringement. Ordered in November 2001 to ensure that no copyrighted material was shared using KaZaA, the company was sold quickly to various interests, including the Australian company Sharman Networks. Subsequent lawsuits in the United States and Australia resulted in settlements of more than $100 million paid by Sharman, Zennström, and Friis.

Their experience with P2P led Zennström and Friis to develop other P2P ventures in 2001, including Joltid, a provider of traffic-optimization and network-management software and the holder of the pair's networking patents, and Altnet, a P2P wholesale network. In 2003 they introduced Skype, a voice-over-Internet protocol (VoIP) application that offered free basic telephone service— including long-distance and international calls—through the Internet, with the firm's earnings coming from fees levied on services (such as voice mail, call waiting, and downloaded ring tones) and imposed on calls placed to land-based telephones. By 2005 Skype had more than 50 million users, principally in Europe and Asia. During negotiations in 2005 with eBay (an online auction Web site) about the possibilities of using Skype to facilitate negotiations between eBay customers on more expensive items, discussions about selling Skype to eBay developed. The deal was soon consummated, with the partners remaining on board, Zennström as CEO and Friis as executive vice president of innovation. eBay agreed to pay them as much as $2.6 billion; more would be paid if Skype subsequently met various performance benchmarks. Zennström and Friis stepped down in 2007, but not before they had made further headlines in 2006 by being named to *Time* magazine's list of the 100 most influential people.

Two years later eBay announced plans to sell Skype, and Zennström and Friis expressed interest in reacquiring the company. They quickly followed up by declaring that the technology behind Skype was leased through Joltid and that they did not plan on renewing the lease. Subsequent maneuvering resulted in Skype's sale in late 2009: majority ownership went to an investor group, while Zennström and Friis acquired a minority stake. In 2011, Microsoft Corporation bought Skype for $8.5 billion.

Their reduced responsibilities after selling Skype in 2005 left Zennström and Friis ample time to pursue other interests, notably Joost, an Internet video service that they founded in 2006. In contrast with YouTube and its heavy reliance on short video clips uploaded by amateurs, Joost offered a wide selection of on-demand television shows from established broadcast and cable television content providers. Unlike Skype, Joost was designed to earn money through advertising, that money being shared with content providers, and, unlike KaZaA, Joost sought to protect copyrighted material for all content providers. A beta (test) version of Joost was made available to invited users in early 2007, and by the time of the official launch in May, Joost's sponsors included the Coca-Cola Company, Intel Corporation, Kraft Foods Inc., Microsoft Corporation, and Nike Inc.

In 2006 Zennström and Friis founded Atomico Ventures, an investment fund that sought out European technology companies that had the potential to be successful in the global market. Zennström and his wife, Catherine, established Zennström Philanthropies in 2007 to support and engage with organizations in efforts to stop climate change and to support human rights. In 2010 Zennström and Friis founded Rdio, a subscription-based music-streaming service.

CHAPTER 41

LINUS TORVALDS

Born Dec. 28. 1969, Helsinki, Fin.

F innish computer scientist Linus Torvalds was the principal force behind the development of the Linux operating system.

At age 10 Torvalds began to dabble in computer programming on his grandfather's Commodore VIC-20. In 1991, while a computer science student at the University of Helsinki (M.S., 1996), he purchased his first personal computer (PC). He was dissatisfied, however, with the computer's operating system (OS). His PC used MS-DOS (the disk operating system from Microsoft Corp.), but Torvalds preferred the UNIX operating system he had used on the university's computers. He decided to create his own PC-based version of UNIX. Months of determined programming work yielded the beginnings of an operating system known as Linux. In 1991 he posted a message on the Internet to alert other PC users to his new system, made the software available for free downloading, and, as was a common practice among software developers at the time, he released the source code, which meant that anyone with knowledge of computer programming could modify Linux to suit their own purposes. Because of their access to the source code, many programmers helped Torvalds retool and refine the software, and by 1994 Linux kernel (original code) version 1.0 was released.

Operating Linux required a certain amount of technical acumen. It was not as easy to use as more popular

Linus Torvalds. Michael Grecco/Hulton Archive/Getty Images

operating systems such as Windows, Apple's Mac OS, or IBM OS/2. However, Linux evolved into a remarkably reliable, efficient system that rarely crashed. Linux became popular in the late 1990s when competitors of Microsoft began taking the upstart OS seriously. Netscape Communications Corp., Corel Corp., Oracle Corp., Intel Corp., and other companies announced plans to support Linux as an inexpensive alternative to Windows. In addition to Linux being free, its source code can be viewed and freely modified by anyone, unlike a proprietary OS. This means that different language versions can be developed and deployed in markets that would be too small for the traditional companies. Also, many organizations and governments have expressed security reservations about using any kind of computer software that contains code that cannot be viewed. For all of the aforementioned reasons, localized versions of Linux have become common in China and many other non-Western countries.

In 1997 Torvalds took a position with Transmeta Corp., a microprocessor manufacturer, and relocated to California. Six years later he left the company to work as a project coordinator under the auspices of the Open Source Development Labs (OSDL), a consortium created by such high-tech companies as IBM, Intel, and Siemens to promote Linux development. In 2007 OSDL merged with the Free Standards Group to form the Linux Foundation.

CHAPTER 42

MARC ANDREESSEN

Born July 9, 1971, Cedar Falls, Iowa, U.S.

American-born software engineer Marc Andreessen played a key role in creating the Web browser Mosaic and cofounded Netscape Communications Corporation.

While still in grammar school, Andreessen taught himself BASIC, a programming language, so that he could write his own computer games; he later attempted to design a program that would do his math homework. He planned on becoming an electrical engineer, but that changed when he entered the University of Illinois at Urbana-Champaign and landed a part-time job at the school's computer lab, the National Center for Supercomputing Applications (NCSA). There, he and a handful of his peers created Mosaic, a user-friendly browser application that integrated graphics and point-and-click simplicity to make it easier for nontechnical people to navigate the Web. Mosaic was a huge success. NCSA made it available free of charge over the Internet, and more than two million copies were downloaded within a year.

After graduating in 1993 with a bachelor's degree in computer science, Andreessen headed to California's Silicon Valley to work for a small company that made security products for use in electronic commerce. Soon he was contacted by James Clark, the founder and former president of Silicon Graphics Inc. Clark was searching for an exciting new venture, and he found it with Andreessen. In April 1994 the duo founded Mosaic

Communications Corporation (later rechristened Netscape Communications). Andreessen recruited the original masterminds behind Mosaic and set out to create the "monster" software, which they initially dubbed Mozilla (meaning Mosaic Killer). It was commercially launched as Netscape Navigator and, almost overnight, became the most popular browser used on the Web, taking over 75 percent of the market share by mid-1996.

Netscape's main objective was to enable individuals and companies around the globe to exchange information. And, as vice president of technology, Andreessen earned the role of setting the company's technical path as it prepared to ride the "bandwidth tidal wave," which Andreessen predicted would transform the wireless communications industry.

The software company reported revenues totaling $55 million for the first quarter of 1996, and that same year Andreessen graced the cover of *Time* magazine. On Feb. 18, 1999, he became chief technology officer at America Online Inc. (AOL), which had purchased Netscape the previous year. Andreessen, however, left AOL after only seven months. He then founded LoudCloud Inc. (later called Opsware), in October 1999; it was acquired by Hewlett-Packard in 2007. In October 2004 Andreessen, along with Gina Bianchini, created Ning, which means "Peace" in Chinese. Andreessen served as chairman of the company, which allows users to create social networks to fit their interests.

CHAPTER 43

JULIAN ASSANGE

Born July 3, 1971, Townsville, Queens., Austl.

Australian computer programmer Julian Assange founded the media organization WikiLeaks. Practicing what he called "scientific journalism" (i.e., providing primary source materials with a minimum of editorial commentary), Assange, through WikiLeaks, released thousands of internal or classified documents from an assortment of government and corporate entities.

Assange's family moved frequently when he was a child, and he was educated with a combination of home-schooling and correspondence courses. As a teenager, he demonstrated an uncanny aptitude with computers, and, using the hacking nickname "Mendax," he infiltrated a number of secure systems, including those at NASA and the Pentagon. In 1991 Australian authorities charged him with 31 counts of cybercrime; he pleaded guilty to most of them. At sentencing, however, he received only a small fine as punishment, and the judge ruled that his actions were the result of youthful inquisitiveness. Over the next decade, Assange traveled, studied physics at the University of Melbourne (he withdrew before earning a degree), and worked as a computer security consultant.

Assange was inspired to create WikiLeaks by Daniel Ellsberg's 1971 release of the Pentagon Papers. Observing that two years had elapsed between Ellsberg's obtaining the Pentagon Papers and their publication in the *New York*

Times, Assange sought to streamline the whistle-blowing process. In 2006 he created the basic design for the site on a computer in Australia, but Wikileaks.org soon moved to servers in Sweden (later adding redundant systems in other countries) because of that country's robust press-protection laws.

Its first publication, posted to the WikiLeaks Web site in December 2006, was a message from a Somali rebel leader encouraging the use of hired gunmen to assassinate government officials. The document's authenticity was never verified, but the story of WikiLeaks and questions regarding the ethics of its methods soon overshadowed it. WikiLeaks published a number of other scoops, including details about the U.S. military's detention facility at Guantánamo Bay in Cuba, a secret membership roster of the British National Party, internal documents from the Scientology movement, and private e-mails from the University of East Anglia's Climatic Research Unit.

In 2010 WikiLeaks posted almost half a million documents—mainly relating to the U.S. wars in Iraq and Afghanistan. While much of the information was already in the public domain, Pres. Barack Obama's administration criticized the leaks as a threat to U.S. national security. In November of that year, WikiLeaks began publishing an estimated 250,000 confidential U.S. diplomatic cables. Those classified documents dated mostly from 2007 to 2010, but they included some dating back as far as 1966. Among the wide-ranging topics covered were behind-the-scenes U.S. efforts to politically and economically isolate Iran, primarily in response to fears of Iran's development of nuclear weapons.

Reaction from governments around the world was swift, and many condemned the publication. Assange became the target of much of that ire, and some American politicians called for him to be pursued as a terrorist. Assange also faced prosecution in Sweden, where he was wanted in connection with sexual assault charges. (It was the second arrest warrant issued for Assange for those alleged crimes, the first warrant having been dismissed in August because of lack of evidence.) Assange was arrested in London in December 2010 and held without bond, pending possible extradition to Sweden.

CHAPTER 44

SERGEY BRIN AND LARRY PAGE

Respectively, born Aug. 21, 1973, Moscow, Russia; born March 26, 1973, East Lansing, Mich., U.S.

On Aug. 19, 2004, Sergey Brin and Lawrence Edward Page went from being promising computer science graduate students to multibillionaire technology mavens when Google Inc., the online search engine company they had founded in 1998, issued an initial public offering of stock that netted each of the entrepreneurs $3.9 billion. By creating the easy-to-use hypertext search engine Google, one of the most successful applications in the history of the Internet, Brin and Page had provided World Wide Web browsing at its simplest to millions of ordinary computer users and had added a new verb, *to google,* to the English language.

Brin moved with his family to the United States in 1979. After receiving degrees (1993) in computer science and mathematics at the University of Maryland, he entered Stanford University's graduate program. In early 1995 he was assigned to show a new Stanford graduate student— Page—around campus. Page had received a computer engineering degree from the University of Michigan before entering the doctorate program at Stanford. By year's end the duo had joined forces.

Brin and Page were intrigued with the idea of enhancing the ability to extract meaning from the mass of data accumulating on the Internet. They began working from Page's dormitory room to devise a new type of search technology, which they dubbed BackRub. The key was to leverage Web users' own ranking abilities by tracking each Web site's "backing links"—that is, the number of other pages linked to them. Most search engines simply returned a list of Web sites ranked by how often a search phrase appeared on them. Brin and Page incorporated into the search function the number of links each Web site had—that is, a Web site with thousands of links would logically be more valuable than one with just a few links, and the search engine thus would place the heavily linked site higher on a list of possibilities. Further, a link from a heavily linked Web site would be a more valuable "vote" than one from a more obscure Web site.

Brin received his master's degree in 1995, but he went on leave from Stanford's doctorate program to continue working on the search engine. In mid-1998 Brin and Page began receiving outside financing (one of their first investors was a cofounder of Sun Microsystems Inc.). They ultimately raised about $1 million from investors, family, and friends and set up shop in Menlo Park, Calif., under the name Google, which was derived from a misspelling of Page's original planned name, googol (a mathematical term for the number 1 followed by 100 zeroes). Brin was the company's president of technology, and Page was chief executive officer (CEO). The partners established an idealistic 10-point corporate philosophy that included "Focus on the user and all else will follow," "Fast is better than slow," and "You can make money without doing evil."

By mid-1999, when Google received a $25 million round of venture capital funding, it was processing 500,000 queries per day. Page stepped down as CEO in 2001 to become president of products. He was replaced as CEO by technology executive Eric Schmidt. However, both Page and Brin remained intimately involved in

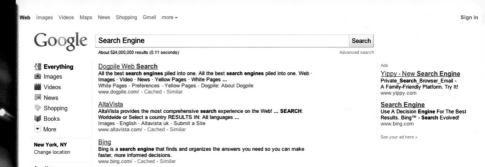

Google was created by Sergey Brin and Larry Page as a means to bring up Internet search results based on the number of links on a site. Pictured is a Google search results page.

running Google. Activity exploded when Google became the client search engine for one of the Web's most popular sites, Yahoo!, and by 2004 users were "googling" 200 million times a day (roughly 138,000 queries per minute). The IPO that year cemented Google's amazing transformation from dorm room hobby to multibillion-dollar technology powerhouse. In 2011 Page became Google's CEO again. Brin, meanwhile, relinquished his duties as president of technology to focus on new products.

CHAPTER 45

JACK DORSEY, "BIZ" STONE, AND EVAN WILLIAMS

Respectively, born Nov. 19, 1976, St. Louis, Mo., U.S.; born March 10, 1974, Boston, Mass., U.S.; born March 31, 1972, near Clarks, Neb., U.S.

In March 2007 social-media entrepreneur Evan Williams, social-networking expert Christopher Isaac ("Biz") Stone, and messaging-software engineer Jack Dorsey released Twitter, an online messaging service that also incorporated aspects of social networking Web sites. By 2009 the service was a media sensation, receiving a Webby Award for Breakout of the Year, and was on its way to becoming a mainstream means of communication adopted and endorsed by celebrities, news outlets, and corporations. Twitter did not charge a fee for its service and had no discernible income, but it was flush with new venture capital, and Williams, Stone, and Dorsey focused on expanding and improving the service. In 2010 the service unveiled "Promoted Tweets" as its intended primary revenue source. Consumers who searched for key words on the service would receive ads from companies that had bought the right to advertise in connection with those words.

Williams grew up on a farm but had aspirations of starting his own business, and he left the University of Nebraska at Lincoln without graduating. In the mid-1990s he briefly ran a company that he and his father set up to provide instructional material about the World Wide Web. He then worked as a Web developer for several California-based computer companies before cofounding (1999) Pyra

Twitter has become so popular that many people post and read "tweets" on their cell phones. AFP/Getty Images

Labs to make project-management software. While he was with Pyra Labs, Williams developed—with Stone—a software tool for publishing personal commentary on the Web. The software, which he called Blogger, formed the basis of a wave of Web logs, or blogs, that soon swelled over the Internet. The new company that Williams had formed, Blogger.com, was bought in 2003 by Google. Williams left Google in 2004 and became a cofounder of Odeo, a podcasting company. Stone joined Odeo in 2005. The following year the men were approached by Dorsey, a software engineer, with the idea of using text messaging and instant messaging (based on the principles of dispatch software) as a way of keeping in touch with friends.

140 CHARACTERS AT A TIME

In a single day a traditional Web log, or blog, might be updated with long entries once or twice, but in that same time period a user of Twitter, the Web's most popular microblogging service, might post dozens of short messages called "tweets"—so long as they are no longer than 140 characters. Twitter works in some ways like an Internet or cell-phone instant messaging service, but it also incorporates features of traditional social networking Web sites such as MySpace and Facebook. Twitter users (alternatively called Twitterers, Tweeters, or simply Twits) could elect to receive the tweets of other posters or track specific topics (marked by a hashtag, the # symbol preceding the term), creating a dialogue of sorts and potentially pushing the number of "followers" in a given Twitter feed into the millions.

Two headline events in 2009 may have transformed Twitter from something that was regarded as an idle hobby for an increasingly wired world into an up-to-the-second news outlet that transcended political borders. On January 15, commuter ferry passenger Janis Krums broke the story of the successful water landing of U.S. Airways Flight 1549 on the Hudson River when he sent out a tweet stating that his ferry was going to rescue people from the downed plane. Krums's hastily snapped camera-phone image of passengers disembarking the half-submerged aircraft was uploaded to Twitpic.com, a photo-hosting service for Twitter users. The site promptly crashed as thousands of Twitterers attempted to view it.

Nowhere was Twitter's role as an emerging outlet for the dissemination of information more apparent than during the events surrounding the Iranian election in June 2009. As state media sources reported that Pres. Mahmoud Ahmadinejad had secured an easy victory, supporters of opposition candidate Mir Hossein Mousavi took to the streets in a series of increasingly violent demonstrations. The topic known as #IranElection became one of the most followed on Twitter as Mousavi supporters coordinated protests and posted live updates of events throughout Tehran. On June 15, three days after the election, Twitter delayed a 90-minute maintenance period at the request of the U.S. State Department, rescheduling it for 1:30 AM Tehran time to avoid interfering with the flow of information within and from Iran. The following day foreign journalists were banned from covering opposition rallies, and Twitter, along with other social networking sites, filled the void left by the traditional media. Government security officers tried to stanch the flow of information by blocking the Web site, while opposition supporters urged #IranElection followers to change their profile settings to the Tehran time zone in an attempt to overwhelm government filters. Events reached a fever pitch following the shooting of Neda Agha-Soltan as she was leaving a protest on June 20. A mobile phone video of the young woman's graphic death was posted on the YouTube video-sharing Web site, and by the following day "Neda" was both the rallying cry of the opposition and one of the top trending topics on Twitter.

With the number of unique visitors increasing some 1,300% in 2009, it was clear that Twitter was more than a niche curiosity. In July the Twitter site was revamped to put a greater emphasis on its expanding role as a source for "what's happening right now, anywhere in the world." As cofounder "Biz" Stone publicly acknowledged later in the year, Twitter had "long outgrown the concept of personal status updates."

Together they developed a prototype of what would become the Twitter platform. The trio then formed a new parent company, Obvious, that acquired Odeo and then spun off Twitter Inc. as a separate entity in 2007. Williams was initially chairman of the board of Twitter, but he moved to the role of chief executive officer (CEO) in late 2008. In 2010 he left that post to concentrate on product strategy.

Stone attended two universities in Boston (Northeastern University and the University of Massachusetts) for one year each and then worked as a designer at Little, Brown and Co. He was creative director (1999–2001) at Xanga, a Web-log community that he had helped form. Williams invited him to take a role in developing Blogger, and Stone joined new owner Google in 2003 but then left (2005) to join Williams in shaping Odeo. After cofounding Twitter, he served as creative director for the company. Stone wrote two books on blogging: *Blogging: Genius Strategies for Instant Web Content*

(2002) and *Who Let the Blogs Out?: A Hyperconnected Peek at the World of Weblogs* (2004). He also served as an adviser to several other Web-site companies.

As a teenager Dorsey created taxi-dispatching software that was adopted by taxicab companies. He attended New York University before moving (1999) to San Francisco, where he set up a company that used the Internet to handle the dispatching of couriers and emergency vehicles as well as taxis. In 2006 he approached Williams and Stone with his short messaging idea and worked with them to develop the prototype. Dorsey served as CEO of the new company until October 2008, when he became chairman of the board. In late 2009 he began beta testing Square, an iPhone device for accepting credit-card payments.

CHAPTER 46

SEAN PARKER

Born Dec. 3, 1979.

A merican entrepreneur Sean Parker was a cofounder of the file-sharing computer service Napster and the first president of the social networking Web site Facebook.

Parker was interested in computers from an early age; his father first taught him computer programming when he was 7 years old. He was arrested at the age of 16 for hacking into the computer network of a major corporation and was sentenced to perform community service. In 1996 he graduated from Oakton High School in Vienna, Va.

American college student Shawn Fanning, a friend of Parker's, devised a program that allowed users to share MP3 copies of music stored on their personal computers over the Internet. Parker, along with Fanning's uncle, persuaded Fanning that the file-sharing program could form the basis of a company, and in 1999 the three founded Napster. In 2001, as a result of a lawsuit by the Recording Industry Association of America, Napster was shut down for illegally distributing copyrighted materials.

The following year Parker and entrepreneurs Minh Nguyen, Todd Masonis, and Cameron Ring founded Plaxo, a Web site that hosted a downloadable software application that served as an online address book for users to collect contact information. Parker was fired from Plaxo in 2004 for his erratic engagement with the company. Interested in the possibilities of social networking, he was intrigued by thefacebook.com (later to become Facebook), a social networking Web site for college students cofounded by Harvard University student Mark Zuckerberg. Parker encouraged Zuckerberg to drop out of Harvard to devote himself to the social network and helped negotiate financing for Facebook from Paypal cofounder Peter Thiel and the venture capital firm Accel Partners. In securing the financing for Facebook, Parker was able to stipulate that Zuckerberg would retain majority control over Facebook's board of directors. Parker became president of Facebook in 2004.

In 2005 Parker was arrested for cocaine possession in North Carolina. No charges were filed, but he was forced to step down as president of Facebook (though he continued to own a minority stake in the company worth hundreds of millions of dollars).

He joined the Founders Fund, a venture capital firm cofounded by Thiel, in 2006 as a managing partner. In 2007 he and activist Joe Green founded Causes, which developed an application for Facebook users to mobilize groups of people for the purposes of advocacy and to solicit donations for philanthropic purposes. (Causes was also a client of the Founders Fund.) In 2010 the Founders Fund invested in Spotify, a Swedish digital music service in which access to its music library was free to users on home personal computers but was available on a paid subscription basis to users on mobile devices. Parker received a seat on Spotify's board and sought to expand Spotify with service in the United States and thus challenge the dominance of Apple's iTunes in the American digital music market.

CHAPTER 47

MARK ZUCKERBERG

Born May 14, 1984, Dobbs Ferry, N.Y., U.S.

American computer programmer Mark Elliot Zuckerberg was cofounder and chief executive officer of Facebook, the world's most popular social networking Web site.

After attending Phillips Exeter Academy, Zuckerberg enrolled at Harvard University in 2002. On Feb. 4, 2004, he launched thefacebook.com (renamed Facebook in 2005), a directory in which fellow Harvard students entered their own information and photos into a template that he had devised. Within two weeks half of the student body had signed up. Zuckerberg's roommates, Dustin Moskovitz and Chris Hughes, helped him add features and make the site available to other campuses across the country. Facebook quickly became popular as registered users could create profiles, upload photos and other media, and keep in touch with friends. It differed from other social networking sites, however, in its emphasis on real names (and e-mail addresses), or "trusted connections." It also laid particular emphasis on networking, with information disseminated not only to each individual's network of friends but also to friends of friends—what Zuckerberg called the "social graph."

In the summer of 2004 the trio moved their headquarters to Palo Alto, Calif., where Zuckerberg talked venture capitalist Peter Thiel into giving them seed money. Zuckerberg dropped out of Harvard to

Facebook started out as a social networking site for Harvard University students and gradually came to be used by people of all ages around the world.
Chris Jackson/Getty Images

concentrate on the fledgling company, of which he became CEO and president. In May 2005 Facebook received its first major infusion of venture capital ($12.7 million). Four months later Facebook opened to registration by high-school students. Meanwhile, foreign colleges and universities also began to sign up, and by September 2006 anyone with an e-mail address could join a regional network based on where he or she lived. About this time Zuckerberg turned down a $1 billion buyout offer from Yahoo!, but in 2007 Facebook struck a deal with Microsoft in which the software company paid $240 million for a 1.6 percent stake in Facebook; two years later Digital Sky Technologies purchased a 1.96 percent share for $200 million. In 2008 Zuckerberg's new worth was estimated at about $1.5 billion.

Success in social networking was not without its perils. In 2007 Zuckerberg was sued for allegedly having misappropriated the idea of Facebook from three Harvard classmates. Three founders of ConnectU, a Facebook competitor, sued in federal court, alleging that Zuckerberg agreed to help finish their Web site but wound up taking their ideas and creating his own site. In what amounted to the refiling of a 2004 lawsuit dismissed on a technicality earlier in 2007, they alleged fraud, copyright infringement, and misappropriation of trade secrets, and they asked the court to shut down Facebook. The next year Facebook settled the lawsuit out of court, but the terms were not disclosed. In 2010, Zuckerberg announced that he would donate $100 million to improve the beleaguered public school system of Newark, N.J.

GLOSSARY

ARPANET (Advanced Research Projects Agency
Network) A network that preceded the Internet
and was based on packet switching, wherein messages were split into multiple "packets" that travelled
independently over many different circuits to their
common destination.

artificial intelligence The ability of a machine to perform tasks thought to require human intelligence.

ballistics The characteristics of flight of a projectile; the
firing characteristics of a firearm or cartridge.

Bernoulli number A rational number that is part of a specific sequence of rational numbers whose relationship
to each other was first determined by Jakob Bernoulli.

binary Relating to, being, or belonging to a system of
numbers having 2 as its base.

Boolean algebra A symbolic system of mathematical
logic that represents relationships between entities—
either ideas or objects.

computer programming language Any of various languages for expressing a set of detailed instructions for
a digital computer.

confocal microscope A microscope in which only what
is in focus is detected, and anything out of focus
appears as black.

differential equation A mathematical statement
containing one or more derivatives—that is, terms
representing the rates of change of continuously vary-
ing quantities.

drawloom A hand loom formerly used for figure weaving.

hashtag The # symbol used by the Twitter service to denote keywords or topics in a Twitter message, or Tweet.

hyperlinking The linking of related pieces of information by electronic connections to allow a user easy access between them.

hypertext A database format in which information related to that on a display can be accessed directly from the display.

infrastructure The underlying foundation or basic framework (as of an organization or a system).

invariance The quality or state of remaining unchanged by specified mathematical or physical operations or transformations.

MP3 (MPEG-1 Audio Layer 3) A data compression format for encoding digital audio, most commonly music. MP3 files offer substantial fidelity to compact disc (CD) sources at vastly reduced file sizes.

prototype An original model on which something is based.

semiconductor One of a class of solids (as germanium, silicon) with electrical conductivity between that of a conductor and an insulator.

switching theory Theory of circuits made up of ideal digital devices, including their structure, behaviour, and design. It incorporates Boolean logic (see Boolean algebra), a basic component of modern digital switching systems.

syntax The way in which linguistic elements (as words) are put together to form constituents (as phrases or clauses).

TCP/IP (Transmission Control Protocol/Internet Protocol) Standard Internet communications protocols that allow digital computers to communicate over long distances.

textile A woven or knit cloth.

transistor Solid-state semiconductor device for amplifying, controlling, and generating electrical signals.

Turing test In artificial intelligence, a test proposed (1950) by the English mathematician Alan M. Turing to determine whether a computer can "think."

BIBLIOGRAPHY

Several of the inventors and innovators profiled in this book wrote memoirs and other works, which are cited in their profiles earlier in the book. Further information can be found in the published biographies and company histories cited in the following text.

James Essinger, *Jacquard's Web: How a Hand Loom Led to the Birth of the Information Age* (2004), recounts what is known about Jacquard's life and then traces the subsequent applications of his punched-card system.

Doron Swade, *The Difference Engine: Charles Babbage and the Quest to Build the First Computer* (2000), by a historian at London's Science Museum, tells the engaging story of Babbage and the first computing machine, with the help of numerous illustrations and photographs.

Dorothy Stein, *Ada: A Life and a Legacy* (1985), analyzes Lady Lovelace's mathematical and scientific work within the context of Victorian science and society.

Desmond MacHale, *George Boole: His Life and Work* (1985), is an accessible biography.

Geoffrey D. Austrian, *Herman Hollerith: Forgotten Giant of Information Processing* (1982); and Robert Sobel, *Thomas Watson, Sr.: IBM and the Computer Revolution* (1981; reissued 2000), are classic biographies of two towering figures from the beginnings of IBM. Kevin Maney, *The Maverick and His Machine: Thomas Watson, Sr., and the Making of IBM* (2003), by a technology journalist, is a more popular biography written with access to previously unavailable company documents.

G. Pascal Zachary, *Endless Frontier: Vannevar Bush, Engineer of the American Century* (1997, reissued 1999), the only existing biography, does an excellent job of weaving together Bush's multiple identities.

Alice R. Burks and Arthur W. Burks, *The First Electronic Computer: The Atanasoff Story* (1988), argues that John V. Atanasoff conceived the first general purpose electronic computer before World War II. Alice R. Burks, *Who Invented the Computer? The Legal Battle that Changed Computing History* (2003), meticulously narrates the patent trial and again favours Atanasoff's over that of John Mauchly and J. Presper Eckert. Conversely, Scott McCartney, *ENIAC: The Triumphs and Tragedies of the World's First Computer* (1999), gives credit to Mauchly and Eckert for designing and building the first fully electronic digital computer in the United States during the war.

Kurt W. Beyer, *Grace Hopper and the Invention of the Information Age* (2009), tells the story of Hopper's life and work, with insight into the status of women in science at the time.

I. Bernard Cohen, *Howard Aiken: Portrait of a Computer Pioneer* (1999), is a life story of the Harvard mathematician who worked with IBM engineers to produce the Harvard Mark I, an early electromechanical computer.

Joel N. Shurkin, *Broken Genius: The Rise and Fall of William Shockley, Creator of the Electronic Age* (2006), recounts Shockley's life and work, through his coinvention of the transistor to his advocacy of views on race and genetics that ruined his reputation. T.R. Reid, *The Chip: How Two Americans Invented the Microchip and Launched a Revolution* (1984; reissued 1986), contains an accessible discussion of Robert Noyce and Jack Kilby and the invention of the integrated circuit. Leslie Berlin, *The Man Behind the Microchip: Robert Noyce and the Invention of*

Silicon Valley (2005), focuses on the man who was awarded the patent for the integrated circuit.

Michael S. Malone, *Bill & Dave: How Hewlett and Packard Built the World's Greatest Company* (2007), is a joint biography of William Hewlett and David Packard as well as a history of the Hewlett-Packard Company, based on numerous interviews and access to company archives.

N.J.A. Sloane and Aaron D. Wyner (eds.), *Claude Elwood Shannon: Collected Papers* (1993), is a good source of information about Shannon and his work. Andrew Hodges, *Alan Turing: The Enigma* (1983, reissued 1992), is a well-written account of Turing's life and his diverse scientific ideas.

Charles J. Murray, *The Supermen: The Story of Seymour Cray and the Technical Wizards Behind the Supercomputer* (1997), balances personal biography, business history, and technology in tracing the development of the supercomputer.

Thierry Bardini, *Bootstrapping: Douglas Engelbart, Coevolution, and the Origins of Personal Computing* (2000), follows Engelbart's personal crusade to make computers usable through the invention of the mouse, the graphical user interface, and other innovations.

Two biographies by computer journalists focus on Apple founder Steven Jobs. Steven Levy, *Insanely Great: The Life and Times of Macintosh, the Computer that Changed Everything* (1994), is a breezy account of the creation of the Macintosh computer and the development of the graphical user interface. Leander Kahney, *Inside Steve's Brain*, expanded ed. (2008, rev. and expanded 2009), analyzes Jobs's management style, accounts for his personal health problems, and profiles other important personalities at Apple, such as chief designer Jonathan Ive.

There are many books about Microsoft and its famous founder. These include the critically minded

James Wallace and Jim Erickson, *Hard Drive: Bill Gates and the Making of the Microsoft Empire* (1993); and the more evenhanded Stephen Manes and Paul Andrews, *Gates: How Microsoft's Mogul Reinvented an Industry and Made Himself the Richest Man in America* (1994).

Glyn Moody, *Rebel Code: The Inside Story of Linux and the Open Source Revolution* (2001), by a computer journalist, is a personal biography of Linux developer Linus Torvalds but also a social chronicle of the free-software movement.

Andrew Lih, *The Wikipedia Revolution: How a Bunch of Nobodies Created the World's Greatest Encyclopedia* (2009), written by a former Wikipedia administrator and containing a short foreword by Wikipedia founder Jimmy Wales, traces the open-source encyclopaedia's evolution and expansion. David Leigh and Luke Harding, *WikiLeaks: Inside Julian Assange's War on Secrecy* (2011), by two British journalists, tells the story of the release of more than 250,000 secret U.S. diplomatic cables to the *Guardian*, the *New York Times*, and other news publications.

Ken Auletta, *Googled: The End of the World As We Know It* (2009); and David Kirkpatrick, *The Facebook Effect: The Inside Story of the Company That Is Connecting the World* (2010), are well-researched company histories by established writers on technology and media.

INDEX